JESUS + SELTZER

Published by The Weight of Ink
www.theweightofink.com

ISBN 978-1-7328987-5-2

Book design by Adam Robinson and Melissa Thornton
Cover art by Daniel Bashta
www.danielbashta.com

JESUS + SELTZER

STORIES + MEDITATIONS
ON SOBRIETY + RECOVERY

JASON UMIDI

The Weight of Ink

Contents

Foreword

by Sandra Coppola

Jason Umidi's book, "Jesus + Seltzer" is honest and inspiring, filled with many personal truths and insight. The author shares a moving and thoughtful glimpse into his recovery process shrouded with hope.

Jason gives a snapshot into his life, offering an invitation for others to compassionately enter the world of freedom in sobriety and recovery and embrace all the hidden rewards it reaps. He so generously invites us into his work, breathing light into a life once filled with behaviors that did not serve him well.

The authors' inspiring and personal thoughts are so eloquently woven into the writings and teachings of various influential people and spiritual leaders. He breathes his own life into their words, finding HIS meaning and HIS understanding. With each thought, he delicately tapped into themes that spoke to basic universal needs—the need to be seen, validated, loved, and accepted without judgment.

Through his understanding, he answers the call to bravely peel back the façade and protective layers that can keep one feeling isolated and alone in their addiction; the self-imposed chains that prevent one from living an authentic life, including the beauty of God's grace. The author skillfully transformed his innermost secrets, thoughts, and behaviors, taking them out of the shadows and into the light of love, hope, and compassion.

Through honesty and self-examination, he finds a subtle way to be of service to others, not preaching or judging but merely by sharing his heart. Humbled by his experience, he embraces his humanness with a deep sense knowing that the shift has occurred for him.

The author leaves us with the call for a compassionate approach and open exploration and stresses that our lives matter and we are never truly alone. He shares the hope that there is joy in true sobriety, finding one's way back into God's arms, and healing of the heart.

Sandra Coppola, Ph.D.
Senior Director, Personal Counseling
Berkeley College

Introduction

Time is really hard to measure. How far can you run in a minute? How well can someone understand your life story in a minute?

How long does it take to read a paragraph? It depends on the reader. You get to be the timekeeper.

Some readers have told me that just one sentence or one key phrase gave them new eyes, new understanding and new hope. It could only have taken a nanosecond, but it lasted for days. It was like their cataracts were dissolved, and they saw the colors of their confusion in the rays of the promised sunrise. For others, it was like an exchange of beauty for ashes. What could it be for you?

Other readers have said that, while reading, their long and winding road came to a fork, and they had the option to choose their direction. As a leadership coach, educator and pastor, I have discovered that too many people never find the redemptive gift of their suffering which could be shared in only a minute. Their daily choices resulted in a lifestyle of becoming more bitter than better. If the authenticity of this book brings greater self-awareness to those of you who are in this place, then that alone is a gift worth receiving.

I have also met those who found that one fellow pilgrim's journey could give them the courage to choose to hope again. After years of disappointment, it could only have happened because the words they stumbled across resonated with their deepest cries, cries that no one else ever heard. It was almost as if a twin brother or sister came back into their life with the news that they had just received a great inheritance, one that would take them out of their emotional and spiritual poverty. Some of you are about to experience a new level of health which is greater than an increase in wealth. The words of this journey could well be the heart of your own.

The real question is, how long does it take to pen these words that you can so quickly consume? It would take an Einstein to come up with a formula, but I can offer my take. How about this: one sentence equals one year, plus one thousand dead ends, plus one million pings of remorse, minus the overwhelming, never-ending, matchless grace of God. It is hard to do the math, but it is easy to see that the end result was worth the wait.

I know that it has been worth my waiting. Like the prodigal father who kept his eyes on the prize of his son's rounding the corner in his long-awaited return home, over thirty years of expectation seems like only thirty minutes when I read these words. These reads are not pep-rally, throw-away comments from motivational speakers that are here today and gone tomorrow. They are heat-seeking missiles to warm cold hearts and breathe life into the dry bones of weariness. They did it for me, and I know they will do it for you.

This is real talk for real times. This book is for those who are hungering to be real and not religious, to be face-to-face vulnerable and not hide behind a mask. This is for those without hope and those with hope that comes and goes. This is for grandparents, parents, children, friends and soon-to-be champions of their own stories. This is for all of those people you will give a copy who will tell you later that it became the gift that kept on giving.

These are not just my opinions. These are the words of someone who has had a front row seat to my amazing son's freedom.

Dad Umidi

Preface

Dear Friend, I've been reflecting lately on my sober journey and the perspective that being clean and sober since January 10, 2017 has given me. Most importantly, some of the truths that I've come to believe based upon my experiences.

But first let me tell you a little bit about how my addictions took over my life and why I'm so passionate about my sobriety. I still remember the first time I got drunk and what a wonderful feeling it was to not feel at all! This magical elixir solved the immediate problem of my pain and evolved into a life of binge drinking. Fast forward a couple of years and I ended up having five back surgeries during the 1990's to fuse my lower spine which left me with a level of chronic pain that has been unbearable at times but constant, nonetheless. The mixing of opioids and Fentanyl with alcohol over the past two decades compounded the deep emotional pain that was buried deep in my psyche. Early childhood trauma left me dead on the inside as I coped the only way I knew how: avoidance and self-medicating.

Raised in the church as a preacher's kid, I knew all about the rules necessary to be a "good Christian" and what that looked like within the church. This performance-based religion only led to a deeper sense of being forgotten by this God I had strived so hard to earn favor with. The loneliness I experienced at my core allowed me to believe the lie of the bottle that told me this was my lot in life, get used to it. Despair and depression worked together to keep me bound for years and left me with zero hope.

I've suffered the typical consequences of being an alcoholic, financial ruin, poor health, divorce, damaged relationships with my current wife and kids, a DUI and wrecked cars but most importantly a deterioration of my personal faith and deep laments with the Creator. Addictions to porn and tobacco also plagued an already tortured soul.

Thankfully this is not the end of the story! How'd I go from this broken and hopeless man to a life full of gratitude? Having sought help through therapy, friends and family over the years, I was still unable to get sober. I eventually woke up one morning feeling the full effects of the mess that I had made of my life and the fact that I was about to lose everything... again. Instead of heading to 7-Eleven for my 7:00 a.m. beer run, I pleaded with God for courage and wisdom. I called the local psychiatric hospital to see if they had a bed in their detox program available. I told my dad that I was an alcoholic and that I needed help and I checked into detox the very next day.

It's been a slow journey but grinding out my sobriety one day at a time has given me the foundation that I enjoy today. Free from the compulsion to drink and use has allowed me to approach the God of my understanding with gratitude and humility. With no regrets or fear of the future, I've settled in for the here and now. To be present in the moment has allowed me to benefit from all the gifts of my sobriety.

The goal in recovery is to be in relationship with one another. To live in truth and honesty with one another. To experience a life that encourages one to grow in love and grace towards those in your family, your circle of friends, co-workers and perhaps that acquaintance you connected with. In fact, ambitious as this sounds, what if we tried to live our lives with the mindset that we are not here on this earth for our own story but for the story of someone else? A simple message of hope and love. Purpose through redemption.

What is the narrative of my journey in recovery? To live recklessly in the moment for truth. To walk in honesty while still feeling like a fraud. To be known as I am. To be called My Beloved. I have to remind myself daily what my priorities are and how I want to implement them. It starts with a simple prayer, "God grant me the serenity to accept the things that I cannot change, the courage to change the things that I can and the wisdom to know the difference."

Probably the biggest hurdle to overcoming my addictions was to tell myself the lie that I didn't need any help. That I'm fine compared to those "other people!" That I can quit anytime I want to. The lies and my pride helped to keep me in bondage. Shame, guilt and the embarrassment that is associated with addictions and the deep depression that I've lived with conspired against me and kept me bound for years.

The good news that I've come to believe is that there is no shame in my flawed self. The years of substance abuse, self-medicating and the reckless behavior…all of it has made me the person that I am today. A day that I'm humbled, appreciative and thankful to be alive. Today is the only day that I've been given and so I must live it with hope and a sense of expectation.

I've learned a few things about hope. A hope that perseveres despite the years of unanswered prayers, when doubts left me angry and confused and the feelings of a death in my spirit. Hope was the only thing that kept me alive over the years. Hope that something has got to change if I just hang in there for one more hour, one more day. The hope that exists when nothing is going your way and when there is silence from the Creator. The weeks, months and even the years where my suffering was not lifted despite all my best efforts. The silence was deafening. Hope is not a feel-good emotion but rather the deep belief that despite the obvious surroundings and my circumstances, God is still pursuing me and has a plan for my life.

Hope is a very important part of my story, and it informs everything that I do. Romans 15:13 says, "May the God of hope fill you with all joy and peace as you trust in him, so that you may overflow with hope by the power of the Holy Spirit." I'm walking out this verse one day at a time and as I follow the path before me, my rough edges will soften, peace and serenity will deepen and a greater sense of purpose and willingness to be of service will continue to grow. I've said this before, but I can't keep what I don't give away. May you be encouraged today and may hope be poured out upon you, a good measure, pressed down, shaken together and running over!

With love,
Jason

THE SERENITY PRAYER

God grant me the serenity
to accept the things I cannot change;
courage to change the things I can;
and wisdom to know the difference.
Living one day at a time;
Enjoying one moment at a time;
Accepting hardships as the pathway to peace;
Taking, as He did, this sinful world
as it is, not as I would have it;
Trusting that He will make all things right
if I surrender to His Will;
That I may be reasonably happy in this life
and supremely happy with Him
Forever in the next.
Amen.

During the addictive years when both alcohol and opioids dominated my life, I no longer believed in dreams. In fact, as I wallowed in the depths of my despair, I had forgotten how to believe. I felt zero hope for my life, and I believed the lie that I was destined to live this way the rest of my days. As my addictions continued to rob me of my sanity, I began to believe that my life was meaningless and that perhaps those around me would be better off without me. Longing for this life to end, to be free from the bondage of alcohol and opioids, I saw suicide as a reasonable escape. The shame and guilt were overwhelming as I tried to reflect on the mess that I had made of my life. Where had everything gone wrong? Why couldn't I make better decisions? To choose life instead of death? I related to what King David wrote in Psalm 42:6, "My soul is downcast within me." I wish I could say that God came down and instantly took away all my pain and restored to me all that I had lost, but that's not been my experience. Instead, I had to put in the work and take those first steps of faith towards sobriety by checking into detox and taking responsibility for the choices that I'd made. Out of the gift of this sober lifestyle, I've reconnected with the spirit within me, and I've been given the opportunity to dream again. My life is full of the joy of my salvation, and the gift of gratitude permeates my entire being. I no longer believe the lie that life is meaningless! Despair no longer haunts me. I'm exactly where I'm supposed to be, and the journey ahead of me is filled with optimism as I begin to dream big dreams. Today, may the Creator God restore you, perfect you, strengthen you and establish you! Do not despair, for God is not finished with you yet!

> Believe that life is worth living and your
> belief will help create the fact.
>
> **WILLIAM JAMES**

This truth was not evident while I languished away in my addictions just a few years ago. In fact, it was quite the opposite, as I struggled to find a reason to keep living. Caught in the endless cycle of substance abuse, my soul lived in a perpetual darkness of the night—a void between the truth that there was a loving God who was pursuing me and the doubts of a broken man unable to believe in hope. How does one navigate through doubt into faith and eventually belief? Little did I know the transformation that would occur simply by getting sober. The physical effects of drying out gave me the energy necessary to continue my sober journey one day at a time. As I focused on gratitude, my mind began to see that the glass was half full and rising. That gratitude then turned into the trust that there really was a plan for my life. This trust opened up my spirit to rest in the grace of the moment. Grace gave me a second chance to believe again. "But I will restore you to health and heal your wounds, declares the Lord" (Jeremiah 30:17). This restoration cleaned the slate, and the wreckage of my past no longer haunts me. This is the promise of the Gospel: that new life can be found in Jesus!

> Sometimes the bravest and most important
> thing you can do is just show up.

BRENÉ BROWN

Showing up for my family wasn't my strong suit during the addictive years. Often, I was too occupied with my own selfish desires to notice the needs of those around me. That all changed on January 10, 2017 when I showed up at detox. That important first step was life changing. Showing up each and every day since getting sober is my offering back to those around me who know and love me. One might say that I was brave in checking into detox, but I didn't feel brave. On the contrary, I felt exhausted, weak, worn out and hopeless that life would get any better. The truth as I experienced it tells me that showing up was the best decision I could've made at that moment, and once I committed to that action, the Lord stepped in, and through His grace and mercy He extended his hand of strength, courage and hope for a restored life. In the *Merriam Webster Dictionary*, restoration is defined as "a bringing back to a former position or condition." According to *Reference.com*, the scriptural meaning of Restoration is to "receive back more than has been lost to the point where the final state is greater than the original condition; someone or something is improved beyond measure." The beauty of being set free from addiction is that just by showing up and doing the hard work, you give permission to the Creator to pour out His restoration upon you. What was unattainable under my own strength has become the bedrock of my sober lifestyle through God's grace and mercy. Show up today, and ask the Lord to meet you where you're at. Trust that His plans for you are perfect, lacking in nothing.

> Let us not look back in anger, nor forward
> in fear, but around in awareness.

JAMES THURBER

During the drinking years, or better yet, the drinking decades, there wasn't a whole lot of self-awareness going on. I was a selfish drinker, putting my needs above everyone else's. The list of grievances that I carried around helped to keep me bound in my addictions, and I failed to take responsibility for my actions, quite often placing the blame on others instead. When I didn't get the response I wanted from others, I pointed my fingers at God as if it was His fault. I was overwhelmed with thoughts of shame and embarrassment, which made it difficult to get the help I needed. However, the very idea of life without a drink, as important as this thought was, terrified me. Humbling myself and finally becoming self-aware was only the beginning of my journey to getting sober. It's no easy task to break the habit, but I found that once I fully committed to the decision, there was no turning back. Step 3 of the 12 Steps of Alcoholics Anonymous says, "Made a decision to turn our will and our lives over to the care of God as we under-stand Him." Herein lies the beauty in getting sober, you don't have to have this God thing figured out. Though still upset with God's seeming lack of care for me regarding my addictions, I nonetheless surrendered what little I had left and asked Him to take the lead. I was sick and tired of being sick and tired, and this was my final attempt at lasting sobriety. When all else fails keep coming back to the Father's love and know that "The Lord is good, a refuge in times of trouble. He cares for those who trust in Him" (Nahum 1:7).

Solitude with God repairs the damage done by
the fret and noise and clamor of the world.

OSWALD CHAMBERS

How often do I really take time for solitude with the Creator?
To listen in silence takes discipline, and my connection to Him
is only as good as the effort that I put into it. But I've found that
when I choose to start my day off with a sense of gratitude, I'm
able to focus more on this relationship with God and less likely to
wander off script. Gratitude may not be an easy action step some
days, but with practice I've found that there is always something
to be thankful for. During the drinking years, I used to see my
cup as always being half empty, but little did I know the rewards
of getting sober would be so numerous. I've found peace and
contentment in my life; while it is often still challenging, the
quality of my life has never been better. Do I still struggle with
health issues? Yes. Difficult relationships? Yes. The mystery of
the Gospel is that "in all these things we are more than conquer-
ors through him who loved us" (Romans 8:37). Today, walk
in the truth that "if God is for us, who can be against us?"
(Romans 8:31).

> Never be afraid to trust an unknown future to a known God.
>
> **CORRIE TEN BOOM**

My future looked bleak on that cold January day when I checked into detox. The only things I knew for sure were that I was an alcoholic and that I needed help to stop drinking. The first step in the Alcoholics Anonymous 12-Step Program says, "We admitted we were powerless over alcohol—that our lives had become unmanageable." What a relief that I didn't have to figure this one out on my own. The really great aspect of submitting to Step 1 is that I get to follow in the shoes of those who've gone before me. Their successes provided the confidence that I needed to commit to this action step. They say, "there's safety in numbers," and this is especially important for those of us who struggle with addiction. Try as I might, I couldn't kick the habit on my own. It wasn't until I humbled myself and was willing to receive this gift given by others that I eventually found lasting sobriety. The fear of the unknown, how to stay sober, caused me much anxiety while going through detox, but Step 2 of the 12 Steps of Alcoholics Anonymous says, "Came to believe that a Power greater than ourselves could restore us to sanity." The Scriptures say in Matthew 19:26, "Jesus looked hard at them and said, "'With man this is impossible, but with God all things are possible.'" It's through God's power that I've come to enjoy this sober lifestyle. Today, may you call upon the God of your understanding, and may you receive the strength that He so generously gives to those who ask.

So long as we imagine it is we who have to look for God, we must
often lose heart. But it is the other way about—He is looking for us.

SIMON TUGWELL

Losing heart was only part of the heartache that I experienced
during the drinking years. Shame, regret and hopelessness were
my more immediate struggles. For me, the truth as I experienced
it was that God's presence was often missing in the depths of
my addictions. For reasons unknown, the Lord remained silent
through most of this journey, or so it seemed. As I sat alone in
the parking lot gathering up the courage to check into detox, I
heard the Creator whisper in my spirit that today would be the
beginning of a life restored. Looking back, He was all around
me, but my heart was deceived in thinking that just because
my prayers were not answered according to my time table that
God was not at work. Jesus rescued me in detox, and it was
out of this first step in humility that the Lord began to reveal
Himself to me. Scripture says in Ezekiel 34:16, "I will search for
the lost and bring back the strays. I will bind up the injured and
strengthen the weak..." Choosing life through detox opened up
my spirit to see the truth that the Lord had been pursuing me
all along. The scales were removed from my eyes, and the act of
grinding out my sobriety one day at a time produced a peace
that transcended all understanding. I'm reminded of the verse
found in Romans 15:13 that says, "May the God of hope fill
you with all joy and peace as you trust in him, so that you may
overflow with hope by the power of the Holy Spirit!" This is the
promise for you today that the God of your understanding will
fill you up with joy, peace and hope!

> Not until we are lost do we begin to understand ourselves.
>
> **HENRY DAVID THOREAU**

My experience in feeling lost while in my addictions over the past couple of decades has led me to today, working out my salvation with fear and trembling. This has been a long journey with much doubt, hopelessness and utter chaos. The mess that I'd made of my life eventually led me to an understanding of myself, but that was not enough, I needed to take action. I'd known for quite a while that I was an alcoholic who was trapped in a vicious cycle of using and abusing substances to escape and to numb the pain both physically and emotionally. Eventually, I became sick and tired, and I was ready for a change. I checked into detox on January 10, 2017, and I've been sober ever since. You don't have to suffer from addiction to know the feeling of being lost. Aren't we all lost to some degree? In an effort to "Know Thyself," I find it necessary to begin each day in thanksgiving, acknowledging the grace that has led me to where I'm at today. Sobriety has taught me to live in the moment, to pause and reflect on where I've come from and in anticipation of where I'm going. The Bible says, "And what does the Lord require of you? To act justly and to love mercy and to walk humbly with your God" (Micah 6:8). Justice, Kindness, Love, Humility! Wow, these are actionable words that I need in my life each day. It's a miracle that I'm even here today, let alone thriving in the love and grace that has been poured out on me. Are you feeling lost? Are you in need of a miracle? May the God of HOPE fill you with all joy and peace in believing, so that you will abound in hope by the power of the Holy Spirit.

> Faith is not being sure where you're going, but
> going anyway. A journey without maps.
>
> **FREDERICK BUECHNER**

Are you on a journey without maps? I know I am. The beautiful part of this quote is that there is no judgment for where your journey is taking you. Since finding lasting sobriety, my journey has taken me through the valleys and to the mountain tops and has opened my eyes to what's possible with a little faith. Hebrews 11:1 says, "faith is confidence in what we hope for and assurance about what we do not see." This is the life we were meant to live! The truth as I'm experiencing it tells me that as I walk out my faith one day at a time, living in the moment, I will not miss out on the joys of this journey. This joy that I have comes from the depths of my soul and was rediscovered through my recovery. Listening to the spirit's still small voice takes discipline, but it's through this action step that I've found love, joy, peace, patience, kindness, goodness, faithfulness, gentleness and self-control. These "fruits" that I enjoy are some of the rewards to living a life of faith. Don't fear the unknown as you journey without maps, rather put your faith in the God of your understanding and trust that He has a plan for your life.

Keep some room in your heart for the unimaginable.

MARY OLIVER

The unimaginable! Wow, this is huge, and I love it! The heart craves the unimaginable deep within its core. In fact, I believe we were created for the unimaginable! Your dreams, desires and relationships are all elements of the heart's yearning for more. To strive towards the seemingly unreachable is the journey that we are all on. For me, the foundation to believing in the unimaginable is born out of the Hope that is found in my faith. To experience hope while everything around me is falling apart is the serenity that my sober lifestyle allows me to experience. To stay in the moment and trust that I'm exactly where I'm supposed to be is life giving. I like what Jeremiah 29:11 says, "'For I know the plans I have for you,' declares the Lord, 'plans to prosper you and not to harm you, plans to give you hope and a future.'" This is the unimaginable, that God sent His son Jesus to die on the cross for our sins, to be raised from the grave so that we may have eternal life through Him. Today, walk in the truth that He is a co-laborer with us as we seek the unimaginable. He knows us intimately and accepts us for who we are. He's our biggest advocate!

> We cannot change anything until we accept it.
>
> **CARL JUNG**

Acceptance is such a difficult task if you're struggling with an addiction. For me, I had to admit that I was powerless over alcohol and opioids and that my life had become unmanageable. Acceptance allowed me a second chance at life. A huge "do over" was taking place, but the hard work was really just beginning. How do you change after decades of addictions? For reasons unknown, my prayers over the years to stop drinking and using were not answered until I fully surrendered and gave my addictions over to the care of God as I understood Him. I couldn't have it both ways. This spiritual journey that I've been on has reshaped my thoughts of who God is and what His desires are. The truth as I'm experiencing it tells me that the Lord desires complete honesty from me, "the good, the bad and the ugly." Honesty opens our hearts to receive. It breaks down the walls that have kept us isolated, and it leads us to repentance. The journey towards recovery requires endurance, but there is a prize at the end! Psalm 40:1-2 says, "I waited patiently for the Lord; he turned to me and heard my cry. He lifted me out of the slimy pit, out of the mud and mire; he set my feet on a rock and gave me a firm place to stand." This is the Good News!

If you would be loved, love and be lovable.

BENJAMIN FRANKLIN

Love, it's what it's all about! Now more than ever should those of us who exercise a personal faith be all about love. Not just for those in our circle, but also for those outside our comfort zones. I don't think I honestly knew how important loving others was until after my sobriety had taken root for a couple of years. You see, being a preacher's kid who was raised in the church, I learned and practiced a lot of "religious" behaviors that blinded me to the needs of those living outside of my experience. I wasn't attuned to the Spirit's calling that I was to love others if I wanted to be loved. Sobriety is such a wonderful gift giver in that I'm always learning something about myself. There is a powerful call from Jesus to His disciples in the New Testament, and it's not about pointing out the sins of others, or about how many blessings one can receive or even the efforts of becoming more righteous, but this: "By this everyone will know that you are my disciples, if you love one another" (John 13:35). Sadly, myself and the church as a whole have often failed those who need the gospel the most—the orphans, the poor, the marginalized, those who do not fit into our worldview of what is or isn't acceptable. The scriptures are full of sound doctrine on what life should look like as a follower of Jesus, but none of it touches the gold standard of being known as people who love others. Without love, our message is empty.

I shall rest and continue to exist.

VIRGINIA WOOLF

Are you finding rest during these trying times? Have you been able to just simply exist? To sit in the moment without any distractions and think on the blessings that you've received? One of the great benefits of getting sober that I've experienced is simple gratitude. Thankfulness for my family, my job and a roof over our head. When gratitude permeates mind, body and spirit, your connection to the God of Creation is strengthened, putting you on solid ground to face whatever life throws your way. Being centered in this living moment has the potential to change one's life, and not just your own, but also the lives of those who know and love you. I believe that as you walk this out you will experience the fruits of the Holy Spirit: love, joy, peace, patience, kindness, goodness, faithfulness, gentleness and self-control. What better gifts to bestow on your fellowman than these fruits?

> Be willing to be a beginner every single morning.
> **MEISTER ECKHART**

I love this quote because it dovetails nicely with how I'm trying to practice my sobriety. Every day I start out forgetting what is in the past, focusing on today and not worrying about tomorrow. I confess that it's not always easy, but the rewards are so worth it. I could never have made it this far in my journey had I not learned humility and how to apply it each morning. The best part about being a beginner each morning is that you are given the opportunity for a fresh start. Perhaps you'll even learn from your mistakes, of which I've made a ton. Herein do we find Grace if we are open to it. Grace that says each morning you are loved by the Creator just by waking up and being you! No performance necessary, no good works, nothing, nada, zilch. It's a free gift to those who are open to receiving it. Romans 11:6 says, "And if by grace, then it cannot be based on works; if it were, grace would no longer be grace." So elegant in its simplicity. May you receive grace today and know that you are loved unconditionally.

> The vision must be followed by the venture. It is not enough
> to stare up the steps; we must step up the stairs.

VANCE HAVNER

Such simple advice, and yet the execution of it can often feel overwhelming if not impossible. My journey towards lasting sobriety started off with me at the bottom step so to speak, looking up at an impossibly tall staircase that seemed unattainable. Our faith journeys are no different. It takes vision to see beyond our circumstances and trust to believe that we are not alone in our journey. I've often said that some of my darkest times were also the loneliest, when the absence of a loving God went on for months, even years. Upon reflection, I can recognize that His presence was all around me, and it's only by His grace that I'm here today to testify to the goodness of the Lord. We all have personal struggles that we keep buried deep within and hope one day will get resolved, but where do we start? Simple steps followed by faith in action allow us to experience the life we were meant to live. Don't settle for the good or the better, but strive for the best that God has to offer you. Destiny awaits those who are willing to lay aside that which hinders them and to listen to the Spirit's still small voice. Scripture says in Proverbs 20:24, "A person's steps are directed by the Lord. How then can anyone understand their own way?" I don't always know where I'm going, but I trust that as I keep putting one foot in front of the other, the Spirit will lead me. As you climb the stairs in front of you today, know that the Creator of the Universe walks with you. He will make known to you the path of life, and in His presence, there is fullness of joy.

> We will not know unless we begin.
>
> **HOWARD ZINN**

As I reflect on my sobriety, it's worth mentioning that there were no guarantees that sobriety would take root, but I had to take that risk. On January 10, 2017, I made the choice to enter detox, creating a paradigm shift that has altered my entire future. Who would've thought that I had joy, peace and hope left in my being? At the time I was unemployed, heavily in debt, with a marriage that was beyond strained. For all intents and purposes, my life was tragically out of control with zero hope. A decision had to be made: was I going to get the help I needed? Detox was just the beginning. Then I needed to take responsibility and follow through with treatment. No more alcohol or prescription opioids, period. Both substances enabled me to ignore my feelings of pain and brokenness. It wasn't just the physical addiction, but, moreover, its band-aid effect, which allowed me to limp through each day lost and in bondage. There is such relief in humbling oneself, realizing that there is a better way to do life. It's never too late to partake in the miracle of Hope! Has life got you down and struggling to cope? Are you too exhausted to carry on another day? Hear this, "Do you not know? Have you not heard? The Lord is the everlasting God, the Creator of the ends of the earth. He will not grow tired or weary, and his understanding no one can fathom. He gives strength to the weary and increases the power of the weak" (Isaiah 40:28-29). Today, receive His total love for you wherever you're at in your journey!

Show up and do the work.

JASON UMIDI

As I continue on my journey of restoration through recovery, I'm reminded daily that you have to show up and do the work. Part of my work was becoming a certified life coach in recovery to best empower those looking to get sober and stay sober. You have to be fearless if you want to choose a life of sobriety; this lifestyle choice takes grit and resiliency. Change happens from within when you set your mind on things that are above. Living with purpose requires that you lead with your heart. Don't be afraid to live this way as this will lead you to your authentic self. That part of you that is one with the Spirit will guide you. This is the way we were meant to live. Let the hypocrisy, self-righteousness and judgment fall to the wayside; hate what is evil, cling to what is good and love with sincerity. Everyone, especially those of us in recovery, is included in those who the Scriptures refer to when Jesus says, "I have come that they may have life, and have it to the full" (John 10:10). How great is that?! Today, there is hope; walk in the knowledge that you are loved with an everlasting love!

> When we are no longer able to change a situation,
> we are challenged to change ourselves.
>
> **VIKTOR E. FRANKL**

Change...When this word challenged me to make the decision to go to detox on January 10, 2017, the fear of the unknown descended upon me like the darkness of the night. Could I really quit alcohol and opioids for good? Fear was masquerading itself when in fact it was an opportunity to change my destiny. Had I given in to this fear and decided against sobriety, I would've missed out on the rich rewards that this sober lifestyle has given me. The fear of change and doing nothing while expecting different results was the insanity with which I was living. Fear and shame had kept me in bondage to my addictions for so long that I sincerely doubted my life was worth living. But wait! That's not the end of the story! Ecclesiastes 3:4 says there is "a time to weep and a time to laugh, a time to mourn and a time to dance." Grace found me, and the season for dancing is now! Life is still complicated, but fear has lost its power over me, and I am no longer settling for what's less than God's best for my life. Isaiah 43:1 says, "Do not fear, for I have redeemed you; I have summoned you by name; you are mine!"

Action is the antidote to despair.

JOAN BAEZ

I love the simplicity of this quote as I'm all about action steps, and this step hits the nail on the head. The despair I felt while trapped in my addictions knew no boundaries. It invaded my entire being. But life presented me with a choice while I was deep in my addictions: to continue doing the same thing, all the while hoping for a different result, or take a blind step of faith towards lasting sobriety. I had zero expectations when I checked into detox, but that small step of humility opened the floodgates of heaven wide and shattered my despair into a million pieces. Regret lost its hold over me as I faithfully walked out my sobriety one day at a time. The glass was no longer half empty, and I began to experience the rewards of choosing this sober lifestyle. So often I can feel paralyzed in my despair, and I'll long for the sweet embrace of hope. Psalm 40:1-2 says, "I waited patiently for the Lord; he turned to me and heard my cry. He lifted me out of the slimy pit, out of the mud and mire; he set my feet on a rock and gave me a firm place to stand." Today, know that there is Hope in Jesus.

> What I see convinces me that God exists;
> what I cannot see, confirms it.
>
> **ALBERT EINSTEIN**

It's been my experience that I don't doubt the existence of God, but I have had difficulty in the past trusting in this mysterious God. Often, what I could not see only left me with more doubt. The unanswered prayers and the failure to find lasting sobriety caused me to turn my back on the Creator as if it was His fault. The good news is that nothing stays the same! I entered into a new season of faith and trust, and I was able to hear clearly the voice of God calling me His beloved while still deep in my addictions. Getting sober was one of the best decisions I've ever made. Submitting to the spirit within, I was able to find the strength to carry on one day at a time until the doubts were removed. Having heard the call of God in my life, I began to write this devotional with the hope that others would find their own source of hope in the living God. Like a mother and her newborn, so too our loving Creator longs to caress us, His children, created in His image to reflect the Love that we've received. This is why "we love because he first loved us" (1 John 4:19).

> *One filled with joy preaches without preaching.*
>
> **MOTHER TERESA**

I'm not a preacher, but I do carry the good news that there is restoration through recovery. I had no idea how much of life I was missing out on just by refusing to give up my addictions. Hope, peace and joy were empty words, and it wasn't until I got clean and sober that I began to see meaning and purpose in my life. There is a saying in the faith community that says, "Let go and let God." My experience is that it can be overused as a passive response, but I believe it's an action step towards the solution. "Letting go" of your addiction is a scary prospect, but don't let fear stand in the way, and, for some of you, the "letting God" part of the equation is even more difficult if not near impossible. Years of unanswered prayers left me cynical of this very phrase, but after I'd been sober for a while, this new way of life and the gratitude that I experienced opened my heart to this mysterious and often complicated God. This is what I know to be true, "Here I am! I stand at the door and knock. If anyone hears my voice and opens the door, I will come in and eat with that person, and they with me" (Revelation 3:20). May you find Him today.

Love pulls people back to their feet. Bodies and souls are fed.
Bones and lives heal. New blades of grass grow from charred soil.

ANNE LAMOTT

Love! This is what I want my faith to be all about. But what is this love? Sobriety has taught me that my love for my fellow man is what it's all about. Having said that, I don't believe that prior to sobriety I really experienced love for others. I was more concerned with serving myself than serving others. I love what Anne Lamott says, "New blades of grass grow from charred soil." This is the HOPE that I'm experiencing! This is the mystery of my faith! That out of total brokenness there is new life. Scripture says in Ezekiel 36:26, "I will give you a new heart and put a new spirit in you; I will remove from you your heart of stone and give you a heart of flesh." This promise is for everyone! That I can find new life in sobriety is the miracle that keeps on giving! How can I ever be the same again? Love transforms! Today, may you go forth and love one another, for love is from God, and whoever loves has been born of God and knows God.

In the darkness of the womb, the future is waiting to be born.

SHANNON CASEY

Though we are living in difficult times with much division and not a whole lot of love going on around us, we can be thankful that there is one who loves us unconditionally. Jesus came into the world to love the deplorables, to love those who would later put Him to death, to love those who scoff at Him and say there is NO God, to love each of us in all of our brokenness. There is nothing that we can do to earn this love, it's a free gift to those who choose to receive it. At times, I find myself doubting this love during the darkness of the soul—those instances of deep depression where there is no relief, no answer and no peace. For whatever reason, my faith journey is filled with these moments of doubt, moments when life seems meaningless and the "joy of my salvation" is just not happening. But I take heart in the fact that these "moments" are just moments; they always pass regardless of their severity, but it takes time and patience. I'm reminded of Mark 9:24, which says, "I do believe; help me overcome my unbelief!" I like this verse because even in our doubts there is room for faith. Today, as you walk by faith and not by sight, may you experience the fullness of God's love and may his peace be upon you.

> It is the nature of desire not to be satisfied, and most
> human beings live only for the gratification of it.
>
> **ARISTOTLE**

This was how I lived my life during the addictive years. Dependence on opioids and alcohol kept me in bondage as I consumed more and more. I was so preoccupied with myself that I wasn't aware of the needs of those around me, and getting sober wasn't even on my radar. I knew I was an alcoholic and an addict, but I thought I could manage my life while holding onto these addictions. But I was deceived in thinking that I couldn't live my life without a drink or a pill, and I traded the truth for a lie when I told myself that I wasn't hurting anyone with my drinking. Eventually, there came a day when I'd had enough. The anxiety was overwhelming as I looked ahead to a life full of unknowns, but Isaiah 41:13 says, "For I am the Lord your God who takes hold of your right hand and says to you, Do not fear; I will help you." It's been a long and difficult journey since getting sober on January 10, 2017, but I wouldn't change a thing. This new lifestyle is deeply satisfying, and I'm full of appreciation for the gift of life. If you're struggling with addiction, hear what the Bible says in 1 Peter 5:7, "Cast all your anxiety on Him because He cares for you."

So much of religion and spirituality that is offered to us is about sanding down the edges. It just so happens that the jagged edges of our humanity are actually what connects us to God and each other.

NADIA BOLZ-WEBER

Wow, I could not have said it any better. As a layman who grew up in a church culture that valued the outward appearance of "right living and smooth edges," I was always trying to attain that standard of external righteousness. While not inherently evil by itself, I felt it was used as a barometer for what mature faith looked like, and the good standing that faith brought in the eyes of God and man. My experience has led me to believe that this culture was one of the biggest reasons for the shame and embarrassment I felt spiritually while I struggled with opioid and alcohol addiction. As a result, I believe the church can be one of the loneliest places for a person struggling with addiction. What a weight that has been lifted since I've embraced my jagged edges. There is freedom in sobriety and through restoration: when your heart is open and your mind is freed, nothing is impossible! Alcoholism is a disease that I wage war against every day, and yes, life still sucks some days, but I wouldn't trade sobriety for anything. There is a path forged by others that can lead you to the freedom that I've found, and if you're struggling with addiction, I encourage you to receive the love and acceptance that a recovery group or a 12 Step program can offer you. Find someone to walk alongside you, and if you're in recovery, share your story with someone else. After all, we as body of people, with all our jagged edges, are the real church, and we are commanded to love one another (everybody, not just those we identify with) as we have been loved! I believe this is the gospel at its best, and there are those in our communities who hunger for this authentic love and acceptance.

> Hope is important because it can make the present moment less difficult to bear. If we believe that tomorrow will be better, we can bear a hardship today.

THICH NHAT HANH

Who doesn't want hope? But how does one find hope in a broken world? I wasn't able to experience this hope until I found sobriety. In my sober journey I've found new life, and the unconditional love from the Lord has set me free. Scripture says in Jeremiah 29:11, "'For I know the plans I have for you,' declares the Lord, 'plans to prosper you and not to harm you, plans to give you hope and a future.'" This promise is for all of us as we work out our salvation one day at a time. To be known and fully loved by the Creator breaks the chains of bondage for those of us who have struggled with addiction. The truth as I'm experiencing it tells me that "there is now no condemnation for those who are in Christ Jesus" (Romans 8:1). This is the Gospel at its best! Nothing can separate you from the love of God. As you go about your day, know that you have an advocate in Jesus who is our comforter and defender.

> The beginning is always today.
>
> **MARY WOLLSTONECRAFT**

How great is this! No matter how much you might've screwed up yesterday or this past weekend, today is a new day! A fresh start to your week is what the Gospel is all about. Scripture says in Lamentations 3:22-23, "Because of the Lord's great love we are not consumed, for his compassions never fail. They are new every morning, great is your faithfulness." During the drinking years, I would awake most mornings in dire straits, forgetting the night before but knowing that, once again, I had drunk too much. My shame prevented me from even going to the Lord and asking for a fresh start. I felt as if I didn't deserve freedom from my addictions, and so I was destined each day to make the same mistakes again and again. Knowing the truth and having grown up in the church, one would think that I of all people, a preacher's kid no less, could access the Scriptures and apply them to my life. But the disease of addiction brands you as being morally bankrupt, unable to live a disciplined life and, quite frankly, "throwing one's life away just for another pill and a drink." Despite the enormous cost of my addictions, I was still deceived in thinking that I wasn't hurting anyone. That I had a problem wasn't even on my radar as I selfishly indulged. The beautiful gift of salvation says that all of this is water under the bridge; we are forgiven, and the record is wiped clean. As far as the east is from the west, so far does He remove our transgressions from us. Today, all of us are offered freedom from our past if you receive the gift of love that is found in Jesus. No quid pro quo. Love, it's what it's all about!

Truth is eternal. Knowledge is changeable.
It is disastrous to confuse them.

MADELEINE L'ENGLE

What I know to be true is that while I was still in the midst of my addictions I was pursued with an everlasting love by the Creator. A love that, quite frankly, I didn't feel or experience until much later in my journey. My experience with truth is that just because you don't believe something doesn't mean it's not true. What I believe is that we have a loving God who pursues each and every one of us with unconditional love. Who desires to be in relationship with us just as we are. No conditions necessary. You are not required to show up in your "Sunday Best" with your life all in order to experience his love, mercy and compassion. Less is more, just show up and be open. Herein lies the rub for those of us trapped in addiction: the shame, loneliness and self-loathing that I felt each time my efforts at sustained sobriety failed sank me deeper into the "unlovable" category. I didn't feel loved, nor did I love myself, and, frankly, I wasn't doing a good job of loving others either. What changed? The compulsion to use and drink was lifted after a long journey through recovery. I began to know and experience the truth that I was loved. Whether you're battling your own addiction or simply living life on your own terms, you are loved with an everlasting love. May you receive God's love today.

> Set your life on fire. Seek those who fan your flames.
>
> **RUMI**

I love this because it's a great reminder that you can't do this life on your own. Trying to quit drinking and opioids on my own was destined to fail, but it wasn't until I entered detox that I realized just how wrong I had been. Step 1 of the 12 Steps of Alcoholics Anonymous states, "We admitted we were powerless over alcohol—that our lives had become unmanageable." Prior to detox, I hadn't put any effort into understanding the 12 Steps, nor did I feel the need to enter the program. On the first night, as I lay on my mat in my room, I swore to myself what a stupid decision I had made by checking into their program. It wasn't until the following morning when I ran into a friend of mine who had also checked in the night before that I fully comprehended that providence was at work in my life. Was I going to be selfish and bail on the program, or was I going to see what God had in store for me? Step 3 says, "Made a decision to turn our will and our lives over to the care of God as we understood Him." Despite being a person of faith, I wasn't living by Step 3 in my personal life. The good news is that my faith is all about second chances! That morning, I had the opportunity to give hope to a friend who was in dire need of friendship. My life was set on fire simply by being available. With all of my doubts, heartaches and anger, I experienced the joy of being of service to someone other than myself. As I gave what little I had, I was refreshed in ways that are difficult to comprehend. But, this is the Gospel at its best. To "love your neighbor as yourself" isn't a suggestion...it's the second commandment after loving God with all your heart, soul, mind and strength (Mark 12:31). Love, it's what it's all about!

> Sometimes we have to do the work even though we don't yet see a glimmer on the horizon that it's actually going to be possible.
>
> **ANGELA DAVIS**

I love this. Another great action step! This sums up for me what our entire faith journey is all about. The Scriptures tell us in Hebrews 11:1, "faith is confidence in what we hope for and assurance about what we do not see." We must do the hard work each day to walk in the hope that our faith produces in us. Listen to the spirit as you face today's challenges knowing that today is all we're promised. To be free from tomorrow's worry or concerns makes all the difference as you try to live in the moment. I could never have gotten sober, nor could I stay sober, if I had to worry about tomorrow. The idea that I can never have another drink is overwhelming if I'm looking down the road, but knowing that today I don't need a drink makes all the difference. The hard work I do today carries me into tomorrow. Don't be afraid of the hard work that awaits you today! Scripture says in James 1:2 "Consider it pure joy, my brothers and sisters, whenever you face trials of many kinds, because you know that the testing of your faith produces perseverance. Let perseverance finish its work so that you may be mature and complete, not lacking anything." Wow, this can be a bit much, but take comfort in the fact that we are promised that the Lord is close to the brokenhearted (Psalm 34:18); He rescues those whose spirits are crushed! Do not lose hope today, but rather walk in the fullness of God's promise that he will never leave you nor forsake you!

> I do not know You, God, because I am in the
> way. Please help me to push myself aside.

FLANNERY O'CONNER

Wow, this quote is so relatable for me. How often during the drinking years did I complain that the God of my understanding was unknowable to me. Even today, when I'm feeling more connected to the Creator than ever before I need help to get myself out of the way. The religious constructs that I've created in my head usually find their way to my heart, and then I'm often lost in my own world. Getting sober was the first step in pushing myself aside, but it's become a daily discipline that I must practice if I'm to be one with the spirit. The truth as I'm experiencing it tells me that God will not push you out of the way, but surrender to him and He will gently lead you. Isn't that a cornerstone of the Christian faith? To say to Abba Father, "… Your will be done on earth as it is in Heaven" (Matthew 6:10). The Gospel is full of examples of great men and women who got in the way of themselves, but the God of all grace and mercy was always ready to step in when they humbled themselves. Surrender to His leading, and rest in the knowledge that the Lord is the same yesterday and today and forever.

Any man may make a mistake; none but a fool will persist in it.

CICERO

This was my life during the drinking years. The constant yielding to my addiction was insanity, and despite the knowledge that I could not sustain this lifestyle, I persisted in it until the very end. I was that fool, and I was an exhausted man who was totally broken and in need of help. The cool part of acknowledging that I needed help was that I had nowhere else to go but up! Detox, Alcoholics Anonymous and one-on-one fellowship were the keys to establishing my lasting sobriety. The Serenity Prayer, "God, grant me the serenity to accept the things that I cannot change, the courage to change the things that I can and the wisdom to know the difference," became my go-to prayer several times a day. As I did the hard work, grinding out my sobriety one day at a time, I began to experience the fruits of these efforts. No longer were my days full of failure, and neither did I experience the shame at the end of each day, but rather my life began to make sense. The glass is no longer half empty. Instead "my cup over-flows," and my days are filled with supernatural optimism that the best is yet to come (Psalms 23:5). Sobriety has taught me to fight for the dreams that are outside of my comfort zone. Dreams that require me to step out in faith with no guarantee that they will be realized. Boldness and courage are gifts from this journey that allow me to embrace my destiny. Isaiah 43:19 says, "See, I am doing a new thing! Now it springs up, do you not perceive it? I am making a way in the wilderness and streams in the waste-land." Today, may you find inspiration and revelation, may you dream big and pursue life to its fullest!

> We thought that we had the answers, it was
> the questions we had wrong.

U2

I love U2's song "11 O'Clock Tick Tock," and this lyric from it reminds me how easily I've gotten things wrong over the years. I've felt confident in the past that I knew what God was trying to do or say in my life or in the life of others only to find out that I was way off the mark. We are human, and we are going to make mistakes, but to me, the invitation in this song is to go deeper. I didn't, nor do I now know, the mind of God, but what of His heart? Is He interested in you? Does He care about you? Does He desire you? Yes, yes, yes! The question may not be why is this happening to me, but where is God in all of this? Do I really trust Him? The truth is He's present in your circumstances today! Every second of every minute the Lord is walking with you, at times He's carrying you while other times He's encouraging you to keep persevering. Scripture says in Deuteronomy 31:8, "The Lord himself goes before you and will be with you; He will never leave you nor forsake you. Do not be afraid; do not be discouraged." I love how simple and complete this verse is. It doesn't try to answer the "why's" that are happening in my life, but it promises me the "where's" so that I may move freely each day in the confidence that I am not alone. Today, know that you are valued just the way you are and that you're pursued by a loving God every step of the way.

I love this quote because it's the only way for me to live nowadays. Having tried it my way for so many years, I've since tried to submit to this very concept in all areas of my life as best as I can. This is especially true as it relates to my sobriety. My experience tells me that to be in the moment and be "all there" requires me to suspend all judgment of the moment and to rest in the security that I'm exactly where I need to be. I remember those early days of sobriety when the desire for a drink was almost all consuming and to sit in the moment was terrifying. I had conditioned my body over the years to always be in "drinking mode," in anticipation of when and where my next drink was going to be. The void that was left once I had removed the alcohol from my lifestyle was huge, and I needed to fill it with something else or my sobriety was not going to last. I've spent the last few years slowly filling that hole with the fruits of my spiritual growth, including the contentment and serenity that they have brought me. Never during my drinking years had I experienced this peace in my life. The freedom from my addictions is positive proof that it can be done! That whatsoever you desire is achievable if you have the courage to take that first step of faith. For me, being in the moment is such a secure place to be, and my hope for each of you, regardless of whether you're struggling with addiction, is that you too can experience this peace. I like what Matthew 7:13 says: "Enter through the narrow gate. For wide is the gate and broad is the road that leads to destruction, and many enter through it. But small is the gate and narrow the road that leads to life, and only a few find it."

> The man who removes a mountain begins
> by carrying away small stones.
>
> **WILLIAM FAULKNER**

Are there mountains in your way today? I'm reminded of the movie *The Shawshank Redemption*, where Tim Robbins' character tunnels out of his cell over the course of 19 years with a small rock hammer, taking pockets full of stones outside and dumping them in the yard. For some of us, the mountains appear to be too large, and the sense in our spirit is that we are overwhelmed by the sheer gravity of the moment. Life is a marathon, not a sprint, so obstacles this large require a long-term plan. For me, the idea of getting sober was years in the making. Once sober, the difficult work began, and the mountain of lasting sobriety looked to be too large for me to scale. But when I decided to take it one day at a time, I was able to string along one sober day, which became two days, and so on. I couldn't have imagined lasting sobriety had I not taken this approach. I'm still carrying away small stones and will do so for the rest of my journey here on earth. The reality is that there are going to be more mountains ahead of you, and unless you have a solid plan of attack, you will continually face defeat. The battle is won in the mind, and to experience success you must find hope in the moment. Hope transforms your vision so that you can see the pathway ahead of you. Most likely, others have gone before you to help prepare the way. Today, know that your mountain is not too big to overcome, and "May the God of hope fill you with all joy and peace as you trust in him, so that you may overflow with hope by the power of the Holy Spirit" (Romans 15:13).

> Showing gratitude is one of the simplest yet most
> powerful things humans can do for each other.
>
> **RANDY PAUSCH**

Prior to getting sober, gratitude was a transactional behavior between myself and another, nothing more and nothing less. What lasting sobriety has taught me is that gratitude is a mindset that I live out 24/7. I now have gratitude for life, family, friends and freedom from addictions. Most importantly, gratitude to the Creator for the opportunity to be of service to my fellowman. Not many people get a second chance to live the life they were meant to live, but I have, and I won't let it go to waste. They say you don't get a second chance to make a first impression, but I disagree. I believe that as one lives out their life with authenticity and loves others as he has been loved, this lifestyle can cover a multitude of sins and speak louder than words. Believe me, my sins were many, but grace found me and extended to me a huge do over! Nothing is as precious as this new life in the Spirit, and this Spirit living has been made available to us by a loving God who desires relationship with us. The good, the bad and the ugly, we are all invited to His table to feast on His goodness, and I promise you that if you seek Him with your whole heart you will find Him. James 4:8 says, "Come near to God and He will come near to you."

An adventure is, by its nature, a thing that comes to us. It is a thing that chooses us, not a thing that we choose.

G.K. CHESTERTON

If I'm honest, sobriety came and found me when I needed it most. This quote found me a few days ago, and my hope is that by writing about it the Creator of the Universe will find ways to work this into someone else's life. We are all on an adventure as we sojourn through this life, but we can't do this on our own. What adventure has chosen you today, and do you need someone to walk alongside you? I couldn't have found lasting sobriety and the gifts that have been given to me had I tried to do it alone. In some respects, sobriety and its adventure found my whole family, and we're on this ride together. Scripture says that "the plans of the Lord stand firm forever, the purposes of His heart through all generations" (Psalm 33:11). I firmly believe that I'm exactly where I'm supposed to be today, and I have no regrets. It's one thing to say I believe in God, but it's another to say that I trust in a loving God. Whatever adventure you're on today, may you put your trust in the God of your understanding and experience His love. 1 Peter 5:7 says, "Cast all your anxiety on Him, because He cares for you."

I love this! It's taken time for me to learn this discipline, but what a difference it's made in my sober journey. As a person in recovery, I find that I need to take time each morning to meditate and pray over my upcoming day. To wait upon the Lord in silence takes practice, but the rewards are so worth it. Because of my sobriety, I get the privilege of experiencing life to its fullest. But it hasn't always been this way. During the drinking years, I chose to argue with most of what my family and friends had to say about my drinking, and instead of choosing wisdom, I allowed myself to be deceived by my arrogance and self-pity. I told myself that my drinking was under control and that I didn't need to quit. Had I understood the value of being silent and really listening, perhaps I could've avoided a lot of the heartache I had put my family through. Eventually, it was through this silence that I finally understood Step 1 of the 12 Steps of Alcoholics Anonymous: "We admitted we were powerless over alcohol—that our lives had become unmanageable." The miracle of Step 1 set in motion is the lasting sobriety that I still enjoy today. Proverbs 2:10 says, "For wisdom will enter your heart and knowledge will be pleasant to your soul." I'm so thankful for the foundation of my faith that has helped me to weather the storms.

> It's not what you look at that matters, it's what you see.
>
> **HENRY DAVID THOREAU**

For a very long time, my glass was always half empty as I often reflected on my failures and regrets. The shame I felt for my failed attempts at lasting sobriety fed the hopelessness that already permeated my spirit. Addictions are these massive roadblocks that prevent you from experiencing the fullness of the spirit for which we were created. Whatever your addiction is—food, sex, porn, alcohol, drugs or something else—there is a pathway towards freedom and restoration. The truth as I've experienced it tells me that once you see and acknowledge that you need help with your addiction, and you begin the humbling path towards recovery, not only does the glass appear half full, but your hopelessness will begin to fade away also. I've learned that if I remove an addiction from my life, I need to fill that void with something else, and for me, that was digging deeper into my faith and drinking lots of seltzer. With sobriety comes spiritual "eyes" that allow you to see the truth that is right in front of you. The gift of restoration through recovery produces hope. Isaiah 40:31 says, "but those who hope in the Lord will renew their strength. They will soar on wings like eagles; they will run and not grow weary, they will walk and not be faint." Your addiction does not define you, it is simply an invitation to go deeper with the Lord who created you. Jeremiah 30:17 says, "'But I will restore you to health and heal your wounds,' declares the Lord!"

> But in times of crisis, the wise build bridges,
> while the foolish build barriers.

KING T'CHALLA

There can be many interpretations of this quote from *The Black Panther*, but for me, it reminds me that one of my purposes in life is to be a messenger of hope. To bridge the gap for those still mired in addiction, doubt and despair. To preach the Gospel that "God is love" (1 John 4:16); that you're valued and accepted just as you are and that there is always hope when you put your trust in the God of your understanding. My spiritual journey through sobriety has taught me many lessons, but the most important one is that you must keep HOPE alive. That the Lord desires honest intimacy with us, his children, and that He has a plan for your life no matter how lost you feel today is the gift of his unconditional love. Here is the good news: Jesus came for all of us while we were sinners, having nothing to present to Him except our brokenness. Despite enjoying a life of freedom from alcohol and opioids, I wake up each day aware that I am fully capable of falling back into my addictions, my doubts, my depression and that overwhelming weight of hopelessness. But I choose to live for today! One day at a time is the only way forward for me! So, put your HOPE in the Lord, for with the Lord there is unfailing love, and with Him is full redemption!

> You do not need to know precisely what is happening, or exactly where it's all going. What you need is to recognize the possibilities and challenges offered by the present moment, and to embrace them with courage, faith and hope.
>
> **THOMAS MERTON**

When I told my dad that I was an alcoholic and that I needed help, I had no idea what my next step was. To be honest, it was all a bit overwhelming and scary, but the truth was out, and now I needed to take advantage of the moment. I immediately checked into a detox program and surrendered my will. That small action step of faith has brought me to where I'm at today, and had you told me this would be my life today I'd have responded with, "Ha! That's crazy talk!" The truth as I've experienced it tells me that we all have within us the courage to take that first step. The late Corrie ten Boom, who with her family hid many Jews in her home during World War II said, "Never be afraid to trust an unknown future to a known God." Whatever that first step is for you today, do not be afraid, and know that the God who has created you knows exactly what you need, and His timing is perfect.

Change can be exciting, or it can be fraught with fear and anxiety. To expect our circumstances to change while doing nothing about it is the definition of insanity. I like Step 2 of the 12 Steps of Alcoholics Anonymous, "Came to believe that a power greater than ourselves could restore us to sanity." Don't we all desire sanity? You don't have to suffer from addiction to experience Step 2, but for us alcoholics, this Step provides us with hope. Hope that has often been deferred while we've suffered alone, often isolated from the ones we love the most. How is it that hope can be so close that you can almost taste it, and yet it eludes many of us for months, even years? For me, the truth as I've experienced it is that Hope has to become an action step. To step out in faith with hope in a power greater than ourselves (for me, that's a loving savior) again and again. You see, for me it took years of seeking to find this lasting hope. Oftentimes, it was two steps forward and one step back, but you keep going hour after hour, day after day, week after week until you see the fruits of your labor. The Bible says in Galatians 6:9, "Let us not become weary in doing good, for at the proper time we will reap a harvest if we do not give up." This is just a season in your life; it won't always be like this. Keep leaning into your struggle, and never give up!

Can these dry bones live again?

JASON UMIDI

I doubted that my broken and dry bones (body, mind and spirit) could one day come alive again. The hope that I'd find a life restored was near impossible for me to believe. The years of addiction and all the baggage that addiction adds to your life created an aura of hopelessness that permeated my entire being. Addiction robbed me of the ability to be in the present moment as I was always living with the regrets of my past. Mentally, addiction is exhausting as you are always looking ahead to the next drink or drug of choice. Shame and self-loathing are the norm for those of us who struggle with addiction. When you add a person's mental illness to the mix, you have the perfect combination of life without meaning or a sense of destiny. But wait! That's not the end! My experience tells me that restoration through recovery is not only possible, but I believe it's promised. Hope can once again flourish as a new heart and spirit dwells within you. This newness of self is the redemptive process that God desires for each of us. Whether you're neck-deep in your addiction or simply living with dead and dry bones, there is hope! God will not abandon you in your time of need, and His spirit will abide in you; renewal, restoration and hope are His gifts to you!

Little did I know when I checked into detox that I would experience a spiritual awakening. All I wanted was the compulsion to drink and use to be lifted. The idea that I had a spirit that could be restored wasn't even on my radar. For me, the consequences of being an alcoholic were such that I lost touch with my spiritual self. The energy that was devoted to maintaining my addictions overwhelmed an already overburdened self. Gone was the security that there was a loving God who had me in the palm of His hands. That I was loved while still in the depths of my addictions didn't seem possible. I had traded the truth for a lie. The perversion of the bottle told me that I was broke beyond repair and destined to live in this bondage the rest of my days. But the Bible says in Romans 8:35, "Who shall separate us from the love of Christ? Shall trouble or hardship or persecution or famine or nakedness or danger or sword?" This is the promise of the Gospel! God's love pierces the messiness of our lives, and it's through this great love of the Father that we are called "children of God!"

> If we pray, we will believe; If we believe, we
> will love; If we love, we will serve.
>
> **MOTHER TERESA**

I love this quote, for it tells of the progression of the Holy Spirit's work in our lives. What a beautiful expression of how prayer works. There were periods in my life over the years where my prayers were selfish, and I missed out on these rewards. As a result, I lost my belief, I did not love and there wasn't any service happening in my life. My addictions prevented me from living the abundant life, and I was effectively reduced to an outsider looking in on the gifts that I was missing out on. But these longings were not enough to spur me into compliance. It wasn't until I surrendered my will and made the decision to pursue sobriety at all costs that I found myself. Finally, I began to experience new beliefs as the scales fell from my eyes. The love that rescued me ignited a spark deep within me that has led me to service. These writings reflect the transformation of a life that once was lost but now is found. Scripture says in Ezekiel 36:26, "I will give you a new heart and put a new spirit in you; I will remove from you your heart of stone and give you a heart of flesh." This is the miracle of grace! Receive the Good News of Romans 8:31: "If God is for us, who can be against us"?!

> Every saint has a past, and every sinner has a future.
>
> **OSCAR WILDE**

I love this quote for its simple truth that we're all a work in progress. Isn't this the gospel at its best?! The promise of redemption for all? Nobody is outside the grip of God's restorative love. I like what Jeremiah 1:5 says: "Before I formed you in the womb I knew you." Think about this for a second. To be fully known and loved today regardless of our past actions is as good as it gets! To those of you who are struggling with addiction, there is hope. Step 3 of the 12 Steps of Alcoholics Anonymous says, "Made a decision to turn our will and our lives over to the care of God as we understood Him." The beautiful part of this Step is that you don't have to have this God thing figured out. Come as you are and be welcomed into His presence. As I sat in detox that first night, I felt the weight of the world on my shoulders. Not even 24 hours sober and yet there I was, asking for a second chance. Scripture promises us that the Lord will never forsake those who seek Him. Little did I know the miracle that was about to happen. While everything was falling apart around me, the Spirit of the Living God visited me in detox and spoke words of truth into my being. "'For I know the plans I have for you,' declares the Lord, 'plans to prosper you and not to harm you, plans to give you hope and a future'" (Jeremiah 29:11). Sober since January 10, 2017, I've been given a new lease on life, and there is no looking back. Today, may you remember that He who began a good work in you will carry it on to completion.

The rule has been disproved. The stone it has been moved.
The grave is now a groove. All debts are removed.

U2

What a comforting thought for me today. Salvation! That all debts are removed is the cornerstone of the Christian faith, and this is available to anyone who asks for it. This is especially true for those of you trapped in isolation with your addiction. The shame of another day living in bondage to alcohol or other drugs is enough to send a person running from the warm embrace of a loving God, but the good news is that the Lord is pursuing us to the ends of the earth. So, here in "Window in the Skies," we have a rock star, Bono, who sings fearlessly of the gospel of grace for everyone through Jesus. Unfortunately, some in the faith community struggle with accepting those addicts and alcoholics who are looking for compassion and support. Often, the disconnect lies in the belief that it's a moral failing rather than a disease. Although it's necessary to tell the addict or alcoholic that God loves them just as they are, that there is Hope in Jesus, we need to show them that same love we've received. Whoever loves God loves others (1 John 4:21). Christ came for all! If you're struggling with addiction today, know that the Lord is good and is present with you in your struggles. He weeps with us; He is a co-joiner in our sufferings. He is abundant in loving kindness to all who call upon Him.

It's impossible for a man to begin to learn what he thinks he knows.

EPICTETUS

This was so true for me during the drinking years. I thought I knew everything. How ridiculous this sounds to me today! I thought I had my drinking under control, not! I thought I could stop whenever I wanted to, not! I wasn't hurting anybody, not! What's crystal clear to me now is that I was deceived by my own selfishness. I was not in a position to "know thyself," and as a result, there wasn't any growth happening in my life. The lies that I told my family and myself kept me in bondage to my addictions, and the shame and regret were overpowering. But how did I transition from being a man with zero hope for achieving sobriety to believing that there was a beautiful plan for my life? Step 1 of the 12 Steps of Alcoholics Anonymous says, "We admitted we were powerless over alcohol—that our lives had become unmanageable." Humility opens up the door for knowledge to be realized. Once I committed to this Step, things started to fall into place for me. One day sober became two, and so on. The success of stringing a few days of sobriety together produced a sense of accomplishment and reinforced the idea that I was on the right path. I "came to believe that a power greater than myself could restore me to sanity," Step 2 of the 12 Steps of Alcoholics Anonymous. For me, this was a loving God who forgave my mistakes and redeemed my life. The simple truth, while difficult to grasp at times, is this, "And we know that in all things God works for the good of those who love him, who have been called according to his purpose" (Romans 8:28). I'm exactly where I need to be today, and I have no regrets! Today, may you walk in the freedom given so generously by a loving God that you too can live without regrets!

> The only way to speak truth is to speak lovingly.
>
> **HENRY DAVID THOREAU**

Man, I love this quote. I may find it difficult to live by this consistently, but the gifts I receive when I do speak lovingly are true. If you're in a relationship or have kids, then you've probably said something truthful that was not well received. In the case of my marriage, I can remember many times when my wife was fed up with my inconsiderate behavior, and no matter how well she spoke the truth in love, my pride would block out the message. The drinking continued, and her words of truth brought more pain as I failed to get sober. One of the saddest consequences of my drinking was that I became a liar to my wife and kids, and, as a result, I was no longer trustworthy. How does this happen? For me, it was a slow descent into a hell of my own making. The selfishness of putting my addictions above my family brought on more shame and regret, and I was slowly spiraling out of control. It was a good spiral though, for it finally brought me to my knees, and I knew I had to do whatever it took to get sober. It's taken time to regain my family's trust, but each day that I'm sober it gets easier. Today, as I choose to speak the truth in love, may I also receive the truth spoken in love.

> The pessimist complains about the wind; the optimist
> expects it to change; the realist adjusts the sails.
>
> **WILLIAM ARTHUR WARD**

I've been adjusting my sails for a while now, but that wasn't always the case. During the addictive years, I was a pessimist in thinking that I'd never find lasting sobriety. The optimist inside of me rarely came out. It's startling to me now as I reflect on those dark days just how little hope I had. It's not that I wasn't aware of Alcoholics Anonymous, but I didn't realize just how straightforward the program was to follow, nor did I really know anyone who openly struggled with addiction. As a result, I felt alone in my shame. This isolation for me was the worst aspect of struggling with my addictions. They say misery loves company, but I'd suggest that those of us who struggle with addiction desire company in a good way. Scripture says in Galatians 6:2, "Carry each other's burdens, and in this way, you will fulfill the law of Christ."

You cannot create experience. You must undergo it.

ALBERT CAMUS

Wow, I love this quote as it's a bold reminder that you can't fake it through this life. You either accept the challenges and grow from them, or you risk losing out on the benefits of submitting yourself to the process. The word "experience" carries gravitas, and you recognize it in someone who has "walked in your shoes," and you trust that person's opinion. Trust is a difficult discipline. Can you trust in a loving God when all you see around you is suffering? Perhaps you're suffering yourself, and it feels like God is nowhere in sight. Hope and faith create trust, and it takes courage to trust in a loving God. In the book *Ruthless Trust* by Brennan Manning, he says, "Trust in God does not presume that God will intervene. Often trust begins on the far side of despair. When all human resources are exhausted, when the craving for reassurances is stifled, when we forgo control, when we cease trying to manipulate God, when we are at our 'wit's ends,' trust happens within us." Trust does not come easily, and, if I'm honest, I've had seasons of doubts and unbelief in my own faith journey. Doubt and faith have co-existed in my life over the years, but as I mature in my faith, doubt is losing its hold over me. Through sobriety, I've encountered a hope that doesn't disappoint. Psalm 34:18-19 says, "The Lord is close to the brokenhearted and saves those who are crushed in spirit. The righteous person may have many troubles, but the Lord delivers him from them all." Today, whatever your experiences are, draw near to the one who has known you and loved you from before creation itself!

Admitted to God, to ourselves, and to another
human being the exact nature of our wrongs.

STEP 5 OF THE 12 STEPS OF ALCOHOLICS ANONYMOUS

Nobody likes confession, especially with another human being, but what an important step if we want wholeness in our lives. This principle of confession is universal and necessary if we are to live life in the spirit. During the addictive years, I held onto grudges way too long, and I was easily offended, especially when my wife tried to talk to me about my drinking. Forgiveness of self was one of the most difficult tasks during my recovery, and before I could forgive others, I first had to undergo this transformation of self. Scripture says in Luke 6:37, "Do not judge, and you will not be judged. Do not condemn, and you will not be condemned. Forgive, and you will be forgiven." Who doesn't want forgiveness? What I found so liberating as I worked on Step 5 was the freedom I found after confession. All the resentment, the hurt and the anger that I had held onto slowly began to fade away as I worked at Step 5 on a daily basis. Confession is the cornerstone to the Christian faith. The Bible says that God "is faithful and just to forgive us our sins and purify us from all unrighteousness" (1 John 1:9). Today, know that you have an advocate with the Father's Son who takes away the sins of all who call upon His name (Acts 2:21).

> There is a crack in everything. That's how the light gets in.
> **LEONARD COHEN**

I've got to be honest—I'm not feeling it today. In fact, it's been a rough couple of days, and the cracks feel like they are about to break me wide open. How is it that you can go from the highest of highs to the lowest of lows in a matter of days? I've learned that I need to double down with my faith during these seasons in my life. Trust that the Spirit is at work within me when I don't feel it. Trust that the Creator has me in His hands, that I am loved by God, that I am His and that He knows me by name (Isaiah 43:1-2). But, I believe these cracks make us human and relatable to each other if we are open to sharing our life journey with others. I think the struggle is not that I have cracks in my life, but whether I will allow them to take over my mind, body and spirit. Perhaps Leonard Cohen had it half right in his song "Anthem," when he wrote, "There is a crack in everything. That's how the light gets in." I would suggest that the cracks in our lives are also meant to let the light shine out! Jesus says in John 8:12, "I am the light of the world. Whoever follows me will not walk in darkness, but will have the light of life." The light of life, I love this! We may never fully know the lives that we impact simply by living an honest and authentic life of faith. Remember we are the light of the world; a city set on a hill cannot be hidden. Who in your life needs to see the light of the spirit in you today?

> Skill to do comes of doing.
>
> **RALPH WALDO EMERSON**

I love the simple discipline of this quote. Just like the iconic Nike® slogan "Just Do It," we must always be moving towards this action step, not away. For me, it's a reminder that I can have all the knowledge of what it means to stay sober, but I have to walk it out each morning. The simple truth for me today is to not take that first drink. I don't worry about tomorrow or next week. As I journey through my sober lifestyle, I'm able to apply this discipline in other areas of my life. Repairing relationships damaged during the drinking years is an ongoing effort that is getting easier the more I practice it. My faith journey is full of "Just Do It" moments. Loving others, serving others and sharing with others all started with this small but important action step. The rewards of practicing this discipline are many. So, if you're struggling with addictions, the promise of freedom from them starts with the simple step of "doing." Step 1 of the 12 Steps of Alcoholics Anonymous says, "We admitted we were powerless over alcohol—that our lives had become unmanageable." I like what Scripture says in Galatians 6:9, "Let us not become weary in doing good, for at the proper time we will reap a harvest if we do not give up." Today, the truth as I'm experiencing it tells me that the Creator of the Universe honors these small steps of "Doing"!

> If you want to get to know God better, get to know God's children.
>
> **S. KLANE**

I really like this quote from *Wisdom, Magic and Miracles*, as it reminds me that my faith has to always be in "action step" mode. To be present in the moment and aware of what God's doing around me. I don't ever want to become complacent in my faith journey, nor take for granted the grace that has brought me this far. I remember my time in detox and the group of individuals that were there looking for lasting sobriety. As broken as we all were, there was a general sense that we were all in this together. We were reduced and stripped from all pretenses, and it didn't matter who you were outside of detox, but who you wanted to become through treatment. Not everyone took advantage of the opportunity, but for those of us who have, it's been the gift that keeps on giving. Even more important than getting sober was the understanding of the value that each person brought to the table. The idea that we are all the same in God's eyes and that He loves each of us equally was a truth that I knew but hadn't really fully grasped until my stay in detox. What a privilege it was to be humbled in that environment. I owe the growth in my spiritual journey to those like me who suffer from addiction. Know today that you are loved with an everlasting love, that this free gift is unconditional. Open your heart and receive it today. Scripture says in Revelation 3:20, "Here I am! I stand at the door and knock. If anyone hears my voice and opens the door, I will come in and eat with that person, and they with me."

Pride makes us artificial, and humility makes us real.

THOMAS MERTON

I don't like anything that's artificial, so it'd make sense that I'd always strive to live humbly in my personal life, but that's not the immediate go-to for me sometimes. Pride is such a crafty animal that it can appear to be an "honest or humble" action or response, but I've learned from some of my past mistakes that you can be fully deceived into thinking your actions are pure. I'm often reminded that humility is actually a place of strength from which we empower those around us to be open and honest. You don't have to suffer from addiction to know that humility puts you on the pathway to spiritual health and wellbeing. Scripture says in Philippians 2:3-4, "Do nothing out of selfish ambition or vain conceit. Rather, in humility value others above yourselves, not looking to your own interests but each of you to the interests of the others." I love this because it lays out for us in simple terms how to serve and love others. The truth as I'm experiencing it reminds me that my message is always Christ through me. It's by Grace that I'm free from alcohol and opioid addiction. The many decades of abuse serve as a daily reminder of just how great a sober life really is. None of which could've been possible had I not humbled myself and asked for help. To live in authenticity requires consistent humility across all of your relationships. Do this today, and enjoy this promise in Psalms 149:4, "For the Lord takes delight in his people; he crowns the humble with victory"! Who doesn't want more victory in their life?!

> The real voyage of discovery consists not in seeking
> new landscapes, but in having new eyes.

MARCEL PROUST

Perspective for me is key to living life with new eyes. Perspective tells me that the feelings of doubt I experience are only temporary. In the past, prior to finding lasting sobriety, the doubts of God's infinite love for me could last for weeks, even months. The doubts that I would ever be free from my addictions lasted for years. How do you transition from doubt to belief? It starts with faith. What is faith? "Faith is confidence in what we hope for and assurance about what we do not see" (Hebrews 11:1). The daily grind of putting one foot in front of the other and at times going two steps forward and one step back finally allowed me to see the light at the end of the tunnel. Scripture says in John 1:5, "The light shines in the darkness, and the darkness has not overcome it." Perseverance in the face of adversity sends roots deep into the soil of your being, allowing you to withstand the periods of silence from the Creator. Quiet meditation has given me the intimate gift of seeing through new eyes. This awareness has freed my tethered soul from the pain and disappointment of my past and connected me to the present where my heart and soul overflows with Hope. This is the beauty of restoration through recovery!

> I prayed for twenty years but received no
> answer until I prayed with my legs.
>
> **FREDERICK DOUGLASS**

I love this quote because it's another reminder I am responsible to do the work. In the film *Bruce Almighty*, Jim Carrey as God is overwhelmed with all the prayer requests that he receives, so he answers everybody's prayer with a "yes," and the ensuing chaos is priceless. When I think of my own prayer requests during the drinking and using years, I picture God shaking his head and saying, "Nope, I don't believe you, Jason, when you say you want to quit. Show me that you're willing to do the work and then come back to me," or something to that effect. During my addictive years, my kids were worried for me, my wife was at her wit's end with me and the consequences of my addictions were not only expensive, but physically, emotionally and spiritually draining. How'd I go from being enslaved to being free? Step 1 of the 12 Steps of Alcoholics Anonymous says, "We admitted we were powerless over alcohol—that our lives had become unmanageable." To surrender is a beautiful action step that allows you to receive from the Spirit a sense of hope that God can and will restore you to sanity. Matthew 11:28 says, "Come to me, all you who are weary and burdened, and I will give you rest."

> What once was hurt, what once was friction, what left a mark no longer stings because Grace makes beauty out of ugly things.

U2

I love these lines from "Grace" by U2 because they relate to my life's journey. When I look back over the last few decades, I can see remnants of this grace thing all around me. There were years where I was intimately aware of how grace kept my head above water as I struggled with my addictions and my faith, but the most telling signs of how grace worked in my life are the times where I didn't see it or feel it at all. That grace was at work in the background of my life is the beauty of the gospel. Looking back, it's a miracle that I'm still here, and I'm so grateful for this sober lifestyle. The ugliness of how addiction destroys lives, families and even generations is evident all around us. But is grace enough? I think so. The first stanza of the song "Grace" goes like this, "Grace,/ She takes the blame / She covers the shame / Removes the stain..." Shame is one of the most debilitating mindsets to overcome if you struggle with addiction, but I believe this grace thing is available to anyone who is seeking redemption and restoration. Regardless of where you're at in your life journey, know that there is freedom in Jesus. This message of grace is not dependent on your good deeds. John 1:17 says, "For the law was given through Moses; grace and truth came through Jesus Christ." Today is a new day; may you experience grace in all of its beauty!

Listen with the intent to understand, not the intent to reply.

STEPHEN COVEY

During the drinking years, this discipline was not accessible as I was too busy trying to justify my selfish actions. How often have I opened up my mouth without really hearing what was just spoken to me? It's not easy to remain silent, but there is maturity in holding back and listening. How often do we sit in the silence of a moment and listen to the Spirit's voice? Or that still small voice of God? Do we really listen, or are we too busy voicing our wants and complaints that we fail to grasp the beauty of these moments? I must confess that I'm often distracted when I sit down to meditate, and when I'm praying, I'll find my mind wandering ahead of me. What I love about my faith relationship with the Lord is that He will drop into my consciousness throughout my day if I'm really listening. To be invited into His presence with all of my brokenness, doubts and unbelief is the beautiful mystery of the gospel. That a sinner like myself can partake in the blessings of knowing my Savior and being fully known and loved by Him is what this love story is all about. Jesus came for all, and He extends his unconditional love to each one of you.

We humbly asked Him to remove our shortcomings.

STEP 7 OF THE 12 STEPS OF ALCOHOLICS ANONYMOUS

I've been on Step 7 for quite some time, it seems. Even now that I've been sober since January 10, 2017, I still have to revisit some of the core steps of Alcoholics Anonymous. It's not enough to ask Him to remove my shortcomings, I need to embrace the truth that I am made whole in my weaknesses. Do I experience doubt and despair on this journey that I'm on? Are there areas in my life that are still broken and in need of the healing touch of the Creator? Am I a work in progress still trying to figure out this abundant life that scripture talks about? Absolutely! Listen to what the Bible says in Matthew 11:28, "Come to me, all you who are weary and burdened, and I will give you rest." All of us, with all of our shortcomings, all of our mistakes and all the mess that we've made trying to make this life livable, are all covered under this promise in Isaiah 41:13, "For I am the Lord your God who takes hold of your right hand and says to you, Do not fear; I will help you." How great is this? If I could communicate one truth today that has been my stronghold on my sober journey it would be this: "Do not fear; I will help you!" May the God of your understanding fill you with all hope as you rest in His unconditional love today!

Justice is not something God has. Justice is something that God is.

A.W. TOZER

Hmm, this sounds really good, but how often are we left with a sense that justice wasn't served? First off, either God is who He says He is, or He's nothing at all. Scripture says in Deuteronomy 10:17-18, "For the Lord your God is the God of gods and Lord of lords, the great God, mighty and awesome, who shows no partiality and accepts no bribes. He defends the cause of the fatherless and the widow, and loves the foreigner residing among you, giving them food and clothing." Is it possible that our definition of justice may need some tweaking? When I think of justice, it's mostly self-centered. Who has wronged me? What do I think I'm entitled to? Often, I'm guilty of not seeing those who are marginalized in our society, who need justice in their own lives. I believe those of us who practice a personal faith should be the first to stand up and give voice to those who have no voice. That's what the Gospel is all about. Jesus says to "love your neighbor as yourself" (Mark 12:31). Who is your neighbor? Read the parable of the Good Samaritan found in Luke 10:25-37. I must confess that prior to finding freedom from my addictions, my spirit wasn't always attuned to the needs of others. It's only been through my recovery that I'm learning how to love others as myself. Love, it's what it's all about.

> Have courage for the great sorrows of life, and patience for the small ones; and then when you have laboriously accomplished your daily task, go to sleep in peace. God is awake.
>
> **VICTOR HUGO**

God is awake! This should be of comfort to those of us who call upon his name in our distress, but what if it isn't? What if our sorrows are still open wounds that just won't heal, and His love is not cutting through the noise in our head? The mornings of despair when I'm in the throes of my depression can leave me empty and void of any hope. I've learned to put one foot in front of the other, but there was a time when even doing that was too much effort. How does one make it through this life without hope? When nothing is going right and everything is hitting the fan, who or what do you turn to? There was a time when I had to have a drink in my hand to face any of life's disappointments and a handful of pills to forget them. But thankfully, those days are no more. I like the lyrics to U2's song, "Drowning Man": "Take my hand / You know I'll be there if you can / I'll cross the sky for your love / For I have promised / Oh, to be with you tonight / And for the time that will come... Hold on, and hold on tightly / Hold on, and don't let go of my love." I've been that drowning man many a time, and will be him again for sure, but there is a lifeline of hope available! "For God so loved the world that he gave his one and only Son, that whoever believes in him shall not perish but have eternal life" (John 3:16). Hold onto his love today and don't let go!

If there is no wind, row.

LATIN PROVERB

A simple statement, and yet profound to me. Over the years I've had great conversations with one of my good friends about prayer and why it so often appears that prayers go unheard or unanswered, and he'd always follow up with, "Yes, but God gave us a brain." At times, I've been the type to sit in the boat praying for wind and wondering why I'm not moving when all along the oars are right by my side. For me, prayer alone did not lift my addictions. I just couldn't get over the hump so to speak until I decided to go "all in." Getting clean and sober didn't happen until I took advantage of all the tools around me. Detox, meetings, disciplined thinking, humility and fellowship with others finally laid the foundation to my sustained sobriety. I've learned over the years to move past the disappointments with God. To be at peace with a life that is different than what I expected or felt that I deserved. To accept the good, the bad and the ugly has been life changing! Today, I'm rowing while still praying for wind.

Out of our collective brokenness, there is a treasure if we have belief in a higher power. For me, that's a loving God who is intimately involved in my daily life. A savior that will redeem my mistakes, restore my spirit, calm my soul and bring me into a right relationship with Him through His son Jesus. My drinking years do not disqualify me from this promise. Once I made the decision to choose sobriety, the Creator of the Universe came to my rescue. From a complicated but simple place of humility and a sense that I had royally screwed up my life, my time had come. On January 10, 2017 when I entered detox, this is the promise that I clung to: "Do not fear, for I have redeemed you; I have summoned you by name; you are mine. When you pass through the waters, I will be with you; and when you pass through the rivers, they will not sweep over you. When you walk through the fire, you will not be burned; the flames will not set you ablaze. For I am the Lord your God" (Isaiah 43:1-2). This pledge is the assurance of God's care for His people. You don't have to do anything to receive this gift except to humbly ask the Creator for faith to believe. 1 Peter 5:10 says, "…the God of all grace, who called you to his eternal glory in Christ, after you have suffered a little while, will himself restore you and make you strong, firm and steadfast." This commitment comes from a God who wishes that no one should perish, but that all should come to repentance. May you find Him today.

> As human beings our greatness lies not so much in being able
> to remake the world...as in being able to remake ourselves.
>
> **MAHATMA GANDHI**

I love this quote because, at its core, it's telling me that there is hope. Second chances, if you will. I'm reminded of the very funny movie *Groundhog Day*, starring Bill Murray and Andie MacDowell. As you may recall, he keeps waking up in Punxsutawney reliving the same day over and over until he finally finds his purpose. His character experiences redemption in the end, and the transformation is inspiring. This is the miracle of Grace! To have the opportunity for a "do over" every morning is a gift unmatched in its value. Sobriety turned a down and out alcoholic like me into a person who cherishes life beyond measure. Those who know me and have followed my journey can testify to the effects of a heart transformed. Out of this restored heart comes the hope to start anew. Scripture says in Ezekiel 36:26, "I will give you a new heart and put a new spirit in you; I will remove from you your heart of stone and give you a heart of flesh." How wonderful is this message? May the God of your understanding fill you with transcendent hope today as you journey in this life.

> Experience is not what happens to a man. It is what
> a man does with what happens to him.

ALDOUS HUXLEY

So true! I love this because it's a reminder to make the most out of our circumstances. Also, there isn't any judgment in the quote for the mistakes that I've made along the way, only the action step to not let them define me. Through my recovery, I've learned that there is nothing wasted in our lives. All the brokenness that we've experienced along the way makes us who we are and informs the way we think and act. I believe we can be made perfect in our weaknesses, and if we can let go of the trauma from our past, our lives can become whole again. I realize this is an ongoing discipline and that we may never "get there," but as long as we make it a part of our daily journey, we will impact others through our story. I've said this before, but we can be the executor of someone's destiny. How great is that? We may never know the influence we've had on a person, but as we live out our lives with authenticity, we get to partner with God as He works in the lives of those around us.

Troubles are often the tools by which God
fashions us for better things.

HENRY WARD BEECHER

I love this quote, but how often do we really look at our life from this perspective? The truth as I'm experiencing it reminds me that, though I made a ton of bad choices during the drinking years, the Lord has redeemed all of it for His glory. Although it's difficult some days when I see the consequences of my drinking still playing out in my life, I'm assured through the Gospel that for those who love God and are called according to his purpose, all things work together for good (Romans 8:28). This is the miracle of my faith: that nothing is wasted from my past, nor does it disqualify me from being a messenger of Hope. The grace that I've received has reshaped my thinking, and I no longer see my past as a liability. Scripture says in 1 Peter 4:10, "Each of you should use whatever gift you have received to serve others, as faithful stewards of God's grace in its various forms." It's a privilege to be a vessel for the transformational power of Grace in one's life and the truth that the Creator longs to be in relationship with us, his children, at all times. This is what it's all about! "God is love, and whoever abides in love abides in God and God abides in Him" (1 John 4:16).

> Even if you're on the right track, you'll
> get run over if you just sit there.
>
> **WILL ROGERS**

What I like about this quote is that it reminds me that there are action steps along my journey that require my attention. Staying sober isn't the end goal as much as being available to assist with someone else's sobriety. The joy that I experience from living a sober lifestyle is only possible through the grace that I find by walking it out one day at a time. To live in community requires one to walk in humility as you serve others. The Bible says in John 15:12, "My command is this: love each other as I have loved you." This is the reminder for me that my sobriety is meant to be shared with others. To love those still trapped in their addiction is the very nature of how God loves me. I can be exactly where I'm supposed to be and still miss out on the miracle if I'm just passively going through the motions. To be available and ready to give a reason for the Hope that lies within me is how I want to start each day. As I live life one day at a time, focusing on the here and now, I'm much more likely to be aware of what the Lord is doing around me so that I may partner with Him to be of service to others. Today as you do life, walk with purpose and be aware of those around you who may need to experience your love and compassion.

*The real voyage of discovery consists not in seeking
new landscapes but in having new eyes.*

MARCEL PROUST

It's critical that we have "new eyes" every morning if we are to walk out our faith journey with authenticity. Whether you're wandering in the desert or climbing up that mountain of hope, trust that the Lord will give you eyes to see and ears to hear. Our faith journey depends upon us listening to that still small voice of the Spirit for guidance and direction. Take the time today to really be content with where you're at in life. Understand that you are exactly where you're supposed to be, and ask for new eyes to see the possibilities that are around you. So often the answer is right in front of us, but we fail to see it. Scripture says in 2 Kings 6:17, "And Elisha prayed, 'Open his eyes, LORD, so that he may see.' Then the Lord opened the servant's eyes, and he looked and saw the hills full of horses and chariots of fire all around Elisha." Despite our humanity and the brokenness that we battle daily, we have hope that in the spirit realm the angels of heaven are doing battle for us in ways we cannot see or understand. Just like in my struggle with my addictions, where it was grace that allowed me to get and stay sober, so too will you be overcomers in your own life. The battle has already been won, we just need the eyes to see the victory that is before us, waiting to be experienced.

> The gift is to the giver, and comes back most to him.
>
> **WALT WHITMAN**

How I love this quote from "Carol of Words" for its simplicity. Give and it shall be given unto you! What better way to start the day than by taking our eyes off of ourselves and focusing them on someone else. My sobriety has taught me that I can't keep what I don't give away. Investing in the life of another person who is struggling with their own addiction keeps me grounded in my own journey. I remember how others poured time and energy into my life during the drinking years, encouraging me to get the help I needed to get sober. The decision to enter detox didn't happen overnight, nor was it a result of one person convincing me to go. Rather, it was a collective effort by many over the years. I'm reminded of the law to love thy neighbor as thy self and how perfect that is as a standalone action step (Mark 12:31). As we love others and support those who are in need, we can experience the miracle of being a gift giver. Sobriety has changed my life, and I'll be forever grateful to those who loved me along the way. As you move through your day, be open to the needs of someone else, knowing that your actions could impact them for years to come.

Don't judge me by my past. I don't live there anymore.

PETTERI TARKKONEN

I love this! However, it can be hard for those of us who are still living with the consequences of making poor life choices, but seriously, what's our alternative? I can't move forward unless I make the decision to forgive and forget. Easier said than done. As a person of faith, I have to look to the scriptures for guidance. The Bible says, "Do not judge, and you will not be judged. Do not condemn, and you will not be condemned. Forgive, and you will be forgiven" (Luke 6:37). We all experience feelings of despair at the mistakes we've made, but hear the Good News in Hebrews 8:12, "For I will forgive their wickedness and will remember their sins no more." If this is the generous gift from a loving Creator for our souls, why can't I let some of my past mistakes be totally forgiven and forgotten? For me, my experience has been that it's the pride in my heart that says I haven't done enough penance to be forgiven. It's a trap that is born out of religiosity and not the Grace that we've received. When I recognize this happening in my thoughts, only then I can move towards Grace again. Today, remember this in 1 John 1:9, "If we confess our sins, he is faithful and just and will forgive us our sins and purify us from all unrighteousness." How great is this? A pardon for all!

Contentment comes not so much from
great wealth as from few wants.

EPICTETUS

Contentment, do you have it? Do I have it? I think so, but it's a daily choice. For me, I'm content because I'm thankful for my sobriety and the life that it's afforded me. No longer am I on the merry-go-round of addiction. I'm content because I have no regrets when I wake up each morning, and what a wonderful feeling that is. My experience with contentment has led me to serve others. Is service to each other not the highest calling? As Mark 12:31 says, to "love your neighbor as yourself"? This love fulfills the law! Knowing how to love in today's polarized landscape is difficult to say the least, but I believe in redemption for everyone, starting with myself. Find that redeeming value, and love like you've never loved before. As Bono of U2 sings in the eponymous song, "Love is bigger than anything in its way!" This love, freely given without expectations, is the gift that will keep on giving.

> The two most powerful warriors are patience and time.
>
> **LEO TOLSTOY**

I love this quote because it's a reminder that when we enter those seasons of doubt, depression, loneliness or hopelessness that we have a solution to our present moment. So often I find myself in a hurry to exit one of these stages, but it's futile if there is a lesson to be learned. To rest in the moment, to be anxious for nothing, takes time and patience (Philippians 4:6-7). This discipline takes courage and trust that the Creator is doing work in your life behind the scenes. Scripture says in Romans 5:3-4, "…we know that suffering produces perseverance; perseverance, character; and character, hope." During the drinking years, I was always looking for a shortcut to finding freedom from my addictions, but what I didn't know at the time was that this freedom had a price. Step 1 of the 12 Steps of Alcoholics Anonymous says, "We admitted we were powerless over alcohol—that our lives had become unmanageable." This is the action step where humility produces the strength necessary to go from perseverance to character, and character to hope. May you find hope in whatever season you find yourself in today, knowing that the testing of your faith produces steadfastness.

> To love another person is to see the face of God.
>
> **VICTOR HUGO**

Seeing the face of God in our fellowman is key if we are to live in true community. I'm reminded again through this quote that it doesn't say to love those who you agree with or those who will love you back. I can struggle at times with this aspect of God's calling. It's not easy loving others, nor should it be! Where's the lesson if it was easy and didn't cost us anything? Anybody can love when it's being returned back to you. I'm talking about an unselfish love. A love that sees the beauty in others. A love that recognizes each other as the children of God. Now more than ever does the world need the light that dwells within us. As you walk in the light, as He is in the light, we have fellowship with one another! Scripture says in Matthew 5:14, "You are the light of the world. A town built on a hill cannot be hidden." As you work out your faith journey, remember that you are loved with an everlasting love. "Whoever does not love does not know God, because God is love" (1 John 4:8)!

> I've learned that people will forget what you
> said, people will forget what you did, but people
> will never forget how you made them feel.

MAYA ANGELOU

How beautiful. I'd expect we would all like to be thought of this way, but how often do we really take the time to make this a reality? I can be so distracted with my own life that I can overlook those closest to me. In fact, how often have I been insensitive to the needs of those around me is an even better statement. My pride and ego will remind me of all the "good" things that I've said, but the truth of the matter is that I must walk the talk. The Bible says in 1 John 3:18, "Let us not love with words or speech but with actions and in truth." The Good News is that "We love because He first loved us" (1 John 4:19). This message of love to our fellowman must reflect the grace that we've received, and in doing so, we can hope for that transforming moment that Maya Angelou has so eloquently expressed. Today, with this purpose in mind, be the person who leaves a lasting mark on someone.

Hope begins in the dark, the stubborn hope that if you just
show up and try to do the right thing, the dawn will come.
You wait and watch and work: you don't give up.

ANNE LAMOTT

One of my favorite authors for sure, Anne has a way of telling
the unvarnished truth with grace and understanding. I appreciate
the simple fact that all she's asking of us while in the darkness is
basically to "show up" and try to do the right thing. Hope doesn't
require us to have it all together—it doesn't matter if you're not
fluent in the scriptures—nor does hope ask that we be full of faith
without any doubt. In fact, I'd say that over the past few decades
of struggling to find hope in my own darkness, I was running on
empty in almost every area of my faith. If I could just manage to
make it through one more day or night, I'd be that much closer
to finding the rest I so earnestly sought. The dawn would always
come, but, most of the time, it didn't bring the relief that I had
been praying for. How do you keep on going when it seems that
your prayers are going unanswered? That the silence you're experiencing as you struggle to find hope is deafening? That the darkness invades both the day and the night? It may seem too much
for you to endure, but the Bible says in Romans 15:13, "May the
God of hope fill you with all joy and peace as you trust in him, so
that you may overflow with hope by the power of Holy Spirit." I
understand that it's not always easy to walk this out, but, at the
end of the day, we're all in this together. True community expresses
itself in love for your fellowman. Try to be the bearer of good news
to those in your life who are desperate for HOPE. It can start out
by simply asking, "How are you?" and letting the moment grow
from there.

> Gratitude makes sense of our past, brings peace
> for today, and creates a vision for tomorrow.
>
> **MELODY BEATTIE**

I've been reflecting a lot lately on gratitude and how it's shaped my worldview these past couple of years. I've said before that my perspective was usually "my cup is always half empty," but out of my struggle with addictions came a sense of peace and joy. A renewed spirit which has given me eyes to see and ears to hear in ways that were near impossible while still in bondage to alcohol. What I like about this quote is that there is no judgment about our past; it is what it is, and I can move forward with understanding. It's also comforting to rest in the moment and to be present in whatever circumstances I find myself in. This "rest" allows my spirit to be open and ready to receive whatever it is that life throws my way. I don't believe that you have to be a person of faith to experience the benefits of gratitude, but taking a step of faith is required in order to accept the gift of gratitude. Especially when life seems unfair and you're struggling with doubt, confusion and hopelessness. I've found life to be more "doable" when I take the time to start each morning with a spirit of thanksgiving. Today, may you receive the gift of gratitude, and, in doing so, pass it along to someone else. Sharing with others is what builds community, and out of this community comes a collective vision for oneness in the Spirit.

> The purpose of freedom is to create it for others.
>
> **BERNARD MALAMUD**

Wow, this really spoke to me this morning. What is freedom? How do we create it for others? I believe it starts with acknowledging the grace in our own lives for the freedoms that we enjoy but didn't necessarily earn. When I reflect on my own freedom from opioids and alcohol abuse, I'm aware of the fact that someone else went before me to prepare the way. I was given the opportunity to choose freedom, but there is a cost to acquiring this gift. Once realized, there is a responsibility for those of us who've experienced freedom in our lives to share it with others. The freedom that I've found from my addictions is a gift that I must give in order to keep it. There is nothing special in the message that I have to share since it's not mine to take credit for. I'm responsible for the decision that I made to choose freedom over bondage, but it's through God's grace that I'm here this morning enjoying the benefits of sobriety. Some of us will continue to struggle in pursuits of freedom and will need the support of those of us who've found it. Take time today to be thankful for the freedoms that you enjoy, and be mindful of those in your life who desperately need to experience this gift. Share with them in their struggles, knowing that we are called to serve one another in love; that's how freedom grows. For the entire law is fulfilled in keeping this one command: "Love your neighbor as yourself" (Mark 12:31).

> That which we persist in doing becomes easier
> for us to do, not that the nature of the thing itself is
> changed but that our power to do is increased.
>
> **RALPH WALDO EMERSON**

I really like this quote for today as it's a reminder that God doesn't necessarily remove our burdens, but He gives us the strength to push through them. Over the years, as religion got in the way of authentic spirit living, I often felt abandoned by God when my prayers were not being answered. It was always about me and what I needed and why I wasn't getting it when I wanted it. As my life spiraled farther out of control and the addictions took over my daily life, I was at a loss as to why my compulsions weren't being lifted. What I learned as I continued to seek lasting sobriety was that, as I continued to put one foot in front of the other and walk out this daily lesson of perseverance, I was being given the strength one day at a time. The greater miracle was not that God came down and rescued me in my time of need, but that through His grace I was redeemed according to His time table. So, if you're in need of that miracle today, and you find that life's not panning out the way you had hoped, don't give up. Don't stop praying, but lean into your circumstances, and know that it's all about the journey and the sanctification that's taking place. Remember that it's through this intimacy with our Creator that we are then able to walk out our life in service to others. "We love because He first loved us" (1 John 4:19).

> To choose hope is to step firmly into the howling wind, baring one's chest to the elements, knowing that, in time, the storm will pass.

DESMOND TUTU

Are you in the midst of a storm today? I like this quote because it gives the action step to choose hope. So much of life is about making a choice, to do or not to do. It doesn't say once the storm has passed then go out; no, we're told to step out now while we're in the middle of it all. Scripture says, "Be strong and courageous. Do not be afraid; do not be discouraged, for the Lord your God will be with you wherever you go" (Joshua 1:9). When you bare your chest to the elements, trust that the Lord will be your stronghold. There is no better shield when facing the storms of life than our loving Creator. There is a reason that we have seasons in our lives, and that's to serve as a reminder that nothing stays the same. Life will continue to evolve in and through you on a daily basis. Keep pressing into the wind, and know that the Lord goes before you to prepare the way. Choose hope today, and don't ever give up!

> Kindness is the language which the deaf
> can hear and the blind can see.
>
> **MARK TWAIN**

Wow, this is so important to remember, especially as a person of faith. We are the mirrors through which people should see the unconditional love that we've received being walked out in kindness to our fellowman. The saying, "You never get a second chance to make a first impression" is so important if we are to walk out our faith in authenticity. Our humanity connects us, but if you're all words and no action, then we all suffer collectively as the body of Christ. Too often, I've not been the first person one would think of to go to when in need of kindness, but, over time, as I've learned kindness from others, it's becoming more natural. Kindness is an active choice that should come naturally for people of faith, and yet there have been times when we as the church have failed miserably at this. I can recall moments of need where all I wanted from the church was kindness and grace, and instead I got a list of "do's and don'ts" and a quick, "I'll pray for you." It's similar to eating out at a restaurant and leaving a Bible tract for your server instead of a generous tip. Trust me, it's happened to me more than once as a waiter decades ago. The point I'm trying to make here is that, out of the Grace that we've received from above, we should be known to everybody as abounding in kindness and grace. Christ said, "By this everyone will know that you are my disciples, if you love one another" (John 13:35).

> I believe that unarmed truth and unconditional
> love will have the final word in reality.
>
> **MARTIN LUTHER KING JR.**

The truth as I'm experiencing it tells me that I don't deserve to be clean and sober. I don't deserve a roof over my head or my loving family. My story alone is useless unless I acknowledge the truth that I'm a product of Grace and the unconditional love that only God can give. I can't add to the story of Christ being born, dying and rising again. This alone gives us life! I've learned this year that I'm no different than the rest of you; my story may be relatable to some of you, but the grace aspect is universal. We all need the Grace that makes us whole and gives us the opportunity to live each new day, not under the law, but under the unconditional love that can only be found through our loving Creator. Regardless of your current circumstances, and however messy your life may seem, there is grace available to you today. Scripture says in Luke 11:9, "Ask and it will be given to you; seek and you will find; knock and the door will be opened to you." Don't bargain with God. Be direct! Ask for what you need!

> Forgiveness says you are given another
> chance to make a new beginning.
>
> **DESMOND TUTU**

I realize that not everyone struggles with addictions like myself, but we are all in need of the great relief that is forgiveness! Whether it's forgiveness in your relationships or forgiveness of self, it's required if you want to live the abundant life. Forget for the moment what religion has taught you and listen to the Good News: "For God so loved the world (you and me) that he gave his one and only Son, that whoever believes in him shall not perish but have eternal life," (John 3:16). A new beginning is what the Gospel is all about, and who doesn't want the chance to start over in some area of your life? Sobriety has been the catalyst to my journey of self-forgiveness. If you're struggling with addiction, Step 3 of the 12 Steps of Alcoholics Anonymous says, "Made a decision to turn our will and our lives over to the care of God as we understood Him." You don't have to have this "God" thing all figured out to start your own journey! Scripture says in Matthew 11:28, "Come to me, all you who are weary and burdened, and I will give you rest"! Today, know that there is nothing that can separate you from His love!

> In order for connection to happen, we have to
> allow ourselves to be seen, really seen.
>
> **BRENÉ BROWN**

We all want connection in our lives, but too often we're not totally comfortable with being fully known. If you had told me on the first day of my sobriety, January 10, 2017, that one day I would share my recovery journey, I would've told you that you were crazy. I had no "legs" yet of what it meant to be sober, let alone to articulate what sobriety could do for one's life. Time has a way of bringing all things into the light if we allow it. Being known takes courage if you're looking to make a personal statement. For me, the truth as I'm experiencing it tells me that to be vulnerable in the "moment," whatever that means to you, simply requires honest living. Let the chips fall where they may, and don't worry about what people will think. Acts 4:13 says, "When they saw the courage of Peter and John and realized that they were unschooled, ordinary men, they were astonished and they took note that these men had been with Jesus." I'm not about religion or doing good works; I'm all about relationship. To be seen, known and fully loved by the Creator is what my sober journey is all about. This lifestyle with Jesus is open to everyone.

Made a searching and fearless moral inventory of ourselves.

STEP 4 OF THE 12 STEPS OF ALCOHOLICS ANONYMOUS

Wow, this is a tough one because it's an ongoing lifestyle choice. This inventory list is a living, breathing document. This isn't some program where at the end of 30 days you've achieved your goals and can move onto something else in your life. Step 4 of Alcoholics Anonymous is, in my opinion, for everyone who desires to live freely in the spirit. To find the peace that comes from honest living. Scripture says in Psalm 139:23-24, "Search me, God, and know my heart; test me and know my anxious thoughts. See if there is any offensive way in me, and lead me in the way everlasting." Getting sober was my fearless first step in my spiritual journey towards wholeness. Restoration through recovery is possible, and as you work out Step 4 above, you will find forgiveness, compassion and new life. What's most important, though, is getting on the road to eternal life. Paul says in Romans 6:23, "For the wages of sin is death; but the gift of God is eternal life in Christ Jesus our Lord." This is the Good News!

I sought my soul, but my soul I could not see. I sought my God, but my God eluded me. I sought my brother and I found all three.

WILLIAM BLAKE

I love this quote because it speaks to the true nature of living in community and its rewards. We can't do this life on our own, and believe me, I've tried. Pride was one of the biggest obstacles to achieving lasting sobriety. Being in community requires authentic living. A life that is open to what others have to teach. An honest and vulnerable spirit that is not afraid to speak the truth in love. Humility that invites others to join the conversation. My experience tells me that service to others begins with loving your neighbor as yourself (Mark 12:31). Out of this love for others you will find the spirit of the living God. Too often, our focus is on loving those who agree with us and those who will love us back, but what if we took the risk to love those who seem unlovable? Why do we love? "We love because He first loved us" (1 John 4:19).

Outrage without an accompanying action turns into paralysis.

SISTER HELEN PREJEAN

You may remember the film *Dead Man Walking* with Sean Penn and Susan Sarandon, for which she won the Oscar for her portrayal of Sister Helen Prejean, a Catholic nun who befriends an inmate (played by Sean Penn) on death row. This quote is an accurate expression of how one person puts her personal faith into action. The spiritual practices of listening, forgiveness and compassion are Biblical themes found throughout this film. I like this quote for its call to action, and if you're a person of faith, I would hope that Sister Helen Prejean's idea of Justice would challenge you to rethink your definition of what moral values are. The whole idea behind "love the sinner, hate the sin" has been so brutally butchered by Christians over the years, myself included, that it's no wonder we've earned the title of being too judgmental! To be honest, I loathe judgmentalism. My entire sober journey is all about trying to be unified with the spirit to show love and compassion to the addict or alcoholic. The shame of being trapped in addiction is enough to cause such despair that even the sweet embrace of a loving Savior can hardly penetrate it. How is it that the church is the last place an addict or alcoholic would turn to for solace? My personal opinion is that we need to do a better job of loving others. I like what 1 John 4:7-8 says: "Dear friends, let us love one another, for love comes from God. Everyone who loves has been born of God and knows God. Whoever does not love does not know God, because God is love." Can it get any simpler?

> Man is born broken. He lives by mending.
> The grace of God is the glue.
>
> **EUGENE O'NEILL**

This is the gospel in its simplest form. Playwright Eugene O'Neill got it right when he said that we are born broken, but that's just the beginning. You don't need to suffer from addiction to know that your life needs mending. In fact, the real test is when life is going great, and you have everything that you need or want in this life. Do you recognize that you're still broken and in need of mending? The Scriptures say that we all have fallen short of God's standard and are in need of a savior (Romans 3:23). There have been numerous times over the years when I felt the harshness and brokenness of life but could not see or feel the presence of the Lord. To struggle in our faith is to be expected, but how do you keep on going when everything seems to be going from bad to worse, and there seems to be no way out? The truth as I've experienced it tells me that, "There is a time for everything…a time to weep and a time to laugh, a time to mourn and a time to dance" (Ecclesiastes 3:1-4). I've learned to be patient in these "mending" moments and to trust in the process. For me, that means I must put one foot in front of the other when all else fails. I've often questioned God on this process, but He reminds me again and again that "this too shall pass."

Start by doing what's necessary, then do what's possible,
and suddenly you are doing the impossible.

SAINT FRANCIS OF ASSISI

My experience over the years has taught me that starting with the impossible has often left me frustrated and hopeless. So it was with my addictions. It's a miracle to be clean and sober, but this miracle started out by accepting the fact that I needed help. No longer could I do what was necessary, let alone the impossible, until I humbled myself and admitted that I was powerless over alcohol. This step was the first of many that got me to where I'm at today. Baby steps of doing the necessary led to success in my quest to be free of my addictions. Having been a slave to them for so long, I'd forgotten what it felt like to be free. Freedom from shame, freedom from regret, freedom from the compulsion to drink and to use, over time all of my burdens lifted as the impossible became the possible. Whether you're struggling with addiction or not, there is freedom in the name of Jesus. Therein is the promise for all of us. John 8:36 says, "So if the Son sets you free, you will be free indeed."

Acknowledgments

How can I begin to show gratitude to the many people who have contributed to my sobriety? It's those who've known me longest, who've seen the arc of my life and the downward spiral, who pleaded with the Lord to intervene. Thank you to my parents, for standing in the gap and praying for me over the years for God's purpose to be fully realized in my life—sobriety being just one of the many prayers lifted up. To my wife, Aimee, for sticking by me when everything looked its bleakest, when all hope seemed to be lost; she still trusted that the Lord was not finished with me yet. To my kids, Cooper, Jessica and Sky, for believing in me and supporting my journey to get whole again, for seeing the best in me even when I couldn't. To the Umidi and DeWeerd families for such unconditional love. To Ken Drinkwalter, for opening the door for friendship and trust to grow that allowed me to live again. To Dr. Mazzio, for giving me the tools necessary to find my way out of the darkness that was enveloping me, which kept me bound both mind and soul. To my good friends, Nick Cokas and Michael Albanese, for friendship that has stood the test of time and for their continued love. To those loyal Facebook friends who've been a part of my daily journey, thank you for your generous comments. To those who've prayed for me from a distance and to those whom I've never met that have interceded on my behalf, this book is for all of you.

Quote Attributions

Photo by George Kartis

About the Author

Jason lives in Norfolk, Virginia with his wife and three kids. Jason is a certified life coach who works with people seeking sobriety. He also has a blog dedicated to the abundant life that can be found in a sober lifestyle at www.todaysoneminuteread.com. Jason is a proud member of the Screen Actors Guild and the American Federation of Television and Radio Artists. While working as an actor in New York City, Jason was also the Director of the New York City branch of Inter-Mission, a ministry out of The First Presbyterian Church of Hollywood that provides support for those in the broader entertainment community. As the host of Third Thursdays, a monthly coffeehouse style gathering, Jason interviewed working actors, producers, writers and models who spoke to the challenges of being a person of faith while navigating a career in the arts. This is Jason's first book for anyone seeking to maintain sobriety, no matter where they are on their personal journey. Find more at jasonumidi.com.

Made in the USA
Middletown, DE
27 September 2022